The Volume Trap

Why fundraising scaled the wrong thing and what comes next

Kevin Schulman

Published by Inflection Press

ISBN: 979-8-9957643-1-1

Table of Contents

Acknowledgements

Most books make it sound like the author had an idea and then wrote it down. That's not what happened here.

Writing a book is an exercise in humility. You think you understand something until you have to explain it clearly to a reader who has no reason to nod politely.

This one took fourteen years of experiments, arguments, failed pitches, successful ones, and a relentless accumulation of evidence before it was ready to be a book. It did not happen alone.

To the clients and organizations who trusted us early, when behavioral science in fundraising was a harder sell than it should have been: this book exists because of your willingness to think differently.

To the DonorVoice team, past and present, who built the tools, ran the studies, survived the pivots, and argued with me productively: your fingerprints are on every chapter.

To the DonorVoice behavioral science team, spearheaded by Kiki Koutmeridou and Stefano DiDomenico — your expertise is unmatched, your commitment to reinventing fundraising even more so.

To Roger Craver, a co-conspirator from the start and mentor who I occasionally blame but mostly credit for bringing me into this world, your commitment to me and DonorVoice is the only reason any of this happened.

And to my wife, Michelle, who for years heard a version of "it's complicated" when asking what I do, this is the longer answer. It turns out it just took a hundred pages plus to explain it properly.

The Volume Trap is an argument for treating donors as human beings. That argument was only possible because a lot of human beings treated me generously along the way.

Prologue: How We Got Here—and How We Get Out

The meeting always goes the same way. Results are flat or down, retention seems stuck or slipping a bit, and without question, acquisition costs are up. Someone flips to the calendar view and points to the obvious solution: more activity. Another mailing, more emails, maybe another matching gift or premium test. Something to boost response before the quarter closes.

No one in the room is cynical, and everyone cares. They're doing what the system has trained them to do. When revenue softens, increase volume. When volume stops working, add urgency. When urgency fades, add something shiny.

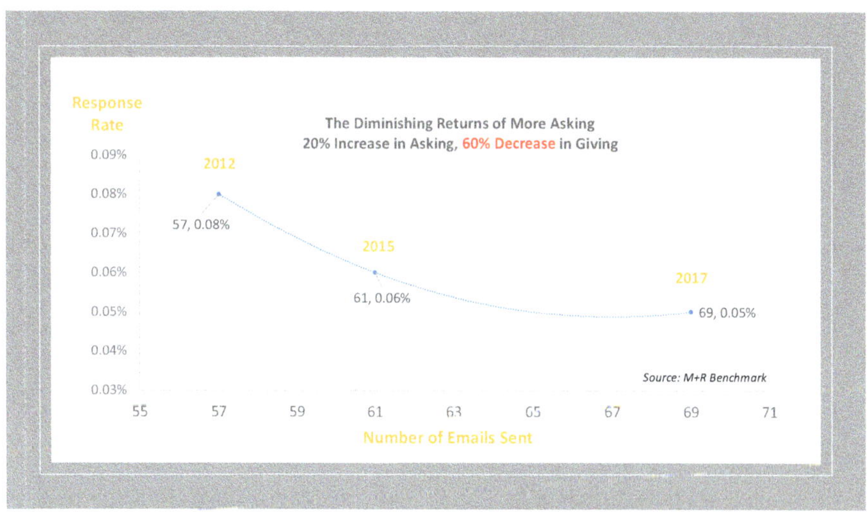

Figure P.1 Email sends and response rate

It feels like strategy because it produces motion.

But motion is not progress. And for a growing number of nonprofits, it is producing the opposite of what it promises (figure P.1).

In 2022, nonprofits sent 15 percent more emails to smaller lists. Conversions dropped 8 percent. Revenue fell 4 percent.

One charity increased mailings from eight appeals a year to eleven, and gross revenue went down. More activity, less return.

It isn't for lack of effort or caring. It's the model: Ask = Give. That seductive assumption has shaped decades of "best practice" into four defaults (Figure P.2) that keep the sector stuck:

Figure P.2 Four Defaults of Volume Machine Model

- **Volume as Strategy**—If asking works, ask more.
- **Sameness for Efficiency**—If asking is the key, reduce workload and send everyone the same thing.
- **Gimmicks as Growth**—When sameness sags, reach for premiums, faux deadlines, and matching coupons.
- **Funnel Vision**—Measure only this month's return.

Volume is the foundation, sameness is the shortcut leading to gimmicks as the reaction, and funnel vision is the mindset that locks it all in place.

The outcome is predictable: shrinking files, falling retention, irritated donors, and fundraisers under pressure to do more of what doesn't work.

The Fix

Asking does not cause giving, any more than a bucket catching rain caused the wet weather. The ask is the mechanism that captures giving when the psychological conditions are right. But the volume machine treats asks as if they create motivation rather than capture it.

The fix requires shifting focus from optimizing the ask to designing the conditions that make people want to give. This means understanding the psychology of why people do what they do, then building a system around that understanding.

The path forward isn't tweaks to the existing system; it's a reboot, a shift to a new, more human model, a human operating system. This system has four interdependent components:

1. **Personalization that isn't skin deep.** Messages must reflect who the donor is, not which customer relationship management (CRM) bucket they're in. Matching the message to the person's values and goals drives resonance in a way "active" and "lapsed" never will.
2. **Motivation designed, not assumed.** Donors keep giving only when the motivation comes from within. External pressure, guilt, or fear may trigger a gift, but they don't sustain one. Even positive emotions like a warm glow fade quickly. What endures is high-quality motivation, and that only comes when giving feels freely chosen, personally meaningful, and effective. When a message satisfies these needs, it fuels commitment. When it doesn't, it chases compliance and burns it out.
3. **Cadence as strategy, not calendar.** Every touchpoint leaves a trace: adstock (positive memory) or irritation (wear-out). Smart cadence means knowing who's ready for more and who needs space, not treating frequency as neutral.
4. **Brand as tomorrow's demand.** Direct response harvests what's ready now; brand plants for tomorrow by building memory associations and recall among the 95 percent of the

market who won't give today. Together, they compound. Alone, each starves.

What This Book Delivers

One simple insight: People do not give because we ask. Understanding why they do is the coin of the realm.

For organizations dialed to eleven on activity, this means ask less, ask better, and raise more. For those with minimal activity, it means backing into frequency rather than starting with it. Either way, "how many asks" isn't the primary lever—it's the by-product of getting the conditions right.

This book shows you how:

- **Part I:** Why the existing defaults keep you stuck
- **Part II:** Personalization that isn't skin deep
- **Part III:** Building a brand that grows demand over time and the metrics required to support it

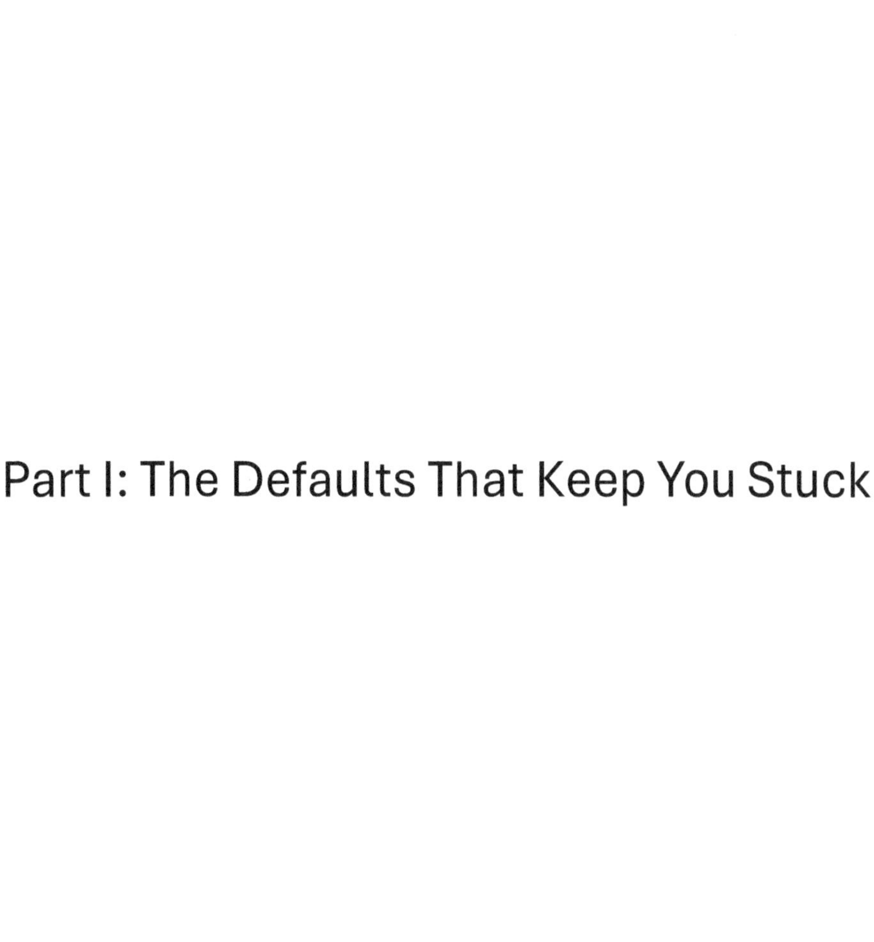

Part I: The Defaults That Keep You Stuck

Chapter 1
The Original Sin: The Ask = Give "Model"

The original sin of fundraising is seductively simple: **If you ask, people will give.**

It looks true. You send an appeal, and dollars come back. The report shows revenue greater than expenses. The board sees a positive return on investment (ROI) and nods in approval. The agency counts another "win." And to be fair, there's truth in it.

But consider this thought exercise: What if you did zero fundraising for a year—what would happen to revenue? It wouldn't go to zero; you'd have legacy gifts, credit card autopay gifts, and habitual end-of-year donors still giving from their mental checklist. This non-zero, baseline revenue (see gray area in Figure 1.1) is currently being miscredited to your fundraising activity.

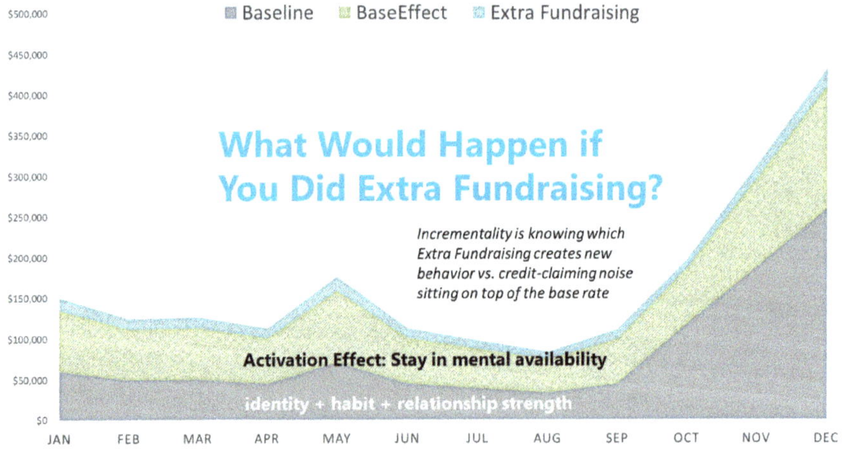

Figure 1.1 Incremental effects of fundraising

Adding *some* fundraising (the green band in Figure 1.1) brings in new dollars on top of baseline; that's the base effect. Some fundraising beats none because it generates *new* behavior, not merely credit stealing from baseline. And the base effect of going from none to some is big. That's the part of the truth every fundraiser sees.

What's harder to see is that piling on more doesn't expand the pie size; it just slices it thinner, accelerates churn, and corrodes motivation.

Why More ≠ More

- **Diminishing returns.** Each additional ask costs the same but produces less. If five appeals generate one gift on average, ten appeals won't generate two. If fundraising really worked like that, every charity would mail a hundred times a year and swim in unrestricted revenue. It doesn't. Instead, the sector has built a system of *reverse -scale* as its best-case scenario: increased activity for less and less return.
- **Cannibalization.** Roughly two-thirds of the revenue from adding an appeal isn't incremental revenue; it's dollars pulled forward. Another thought exercise: How many of your appeals would be net positive if you subtracted 65 percent from the gross revenue line? We're robbing Peter to pay Paul, so the pie doesn't grow; we just cut tomorrow's slice today.
- **Donor cadence.** Most donors don't give again, roughly 60 percent by our estimates. The next most likely behavior pattern is one gift per year, no matter how often you ask. You can send four or four hundred appeals; they'll still only give once. Push harder, and you risk moving them from one to none.

Together, these three truths explain why "ask more = raise more" is a lie fundraisers are taught to believe. The revenue > expense on a single appeal may look like proof, but in reality, it's a mix of diminishing returns, cannibalized dollars, and donors who were never going to respond more than once in the first place.

The Corrosion of Motivation

If diminishing returns and cannibalization were the only problems, the volume model would merely be inefficient. The bigger danger is what constant asking does to people.

Psychology has long shown that when people feel controlled, pressured, or nagged, their motivation shifts. It moves from intrinsic ("I want to do this") to extrinsic ("I'm doing this to get you off my back"). Once that shift happens, the behavior becomes fragile.

Fundraising is no different. When every interaction is an ask, donors don't feel invited; they feel pursued.

It shows up in two ways:

- **Irritation.** Decades of advertising research show a consistent curve: Exposure helps at first, then plateaus, then irritates. The same dynamic holds in fundraising. Donors rarely call to complain; they simply tune out. It's a quiet disengagement, a mental unsubscribe.
- **Erosion of loyalty.** If volume created loyalty, retention would rise with frequency. Instead, nearly three out of four donors vanish after their first or second gift. More contact doesn't deepen commitment; it accelerates attrition as donors feel underappreciated and as if no amount of giving will be enough.

This is the paradox of volume: The very thing meant to drive giving corrodes the desire to give.

Volume doesn't just fail to create new value. It destroys the value you already have.

Why the Machine Keeps Running

If the evidence is so clear, why hasn't the model changed? Because the system is wired to reward activity, not outcomes.

Agencies and vendors mark up production costs and take commissions on media spend. List brokers make money on every name rented.

Printers profit from every additional drop. In this model, every incremental appeal guarantees one thing: The agency and vendor side makes more. Your mission? Not so much.

The incentives are misaligned, keeping the treadmill running, even as donors quietly step off. The “ask more = raise more” model isn’t growth. It’s collapse, playing out in slow motion.

And if asking more often is the first blind spot, treating every donor as if they’re the same is the second, as covered in the next chapter.

Chapter 2
Original Sin Compounded: One-Size-Fits-All Approach

If you believe asking creates giving, then *what* you send doesn't really matter. Just ask, and dollars appear. That's why sameness is the natural extension of volume. If asking is the cause, then every donor gets the same thing. Why bother tailoring at all?

And so, fundraising's second default took root: *One- size- fits- all.*

The Illusion of Optimization

Even our most celebrated discipline, testing, reinforces sameness. We write two versions of an appeal, split the file, and see which one "wins." On the surface, it looks rigorous, data-driven, sophisticated.

But the logic underneath is sameness.

It's like serving two dishes to a crowded restaurant without asking who ordered what. Whichever dish gets more total bites becomes the only item on the menu. Some diners loved it; some hated it. You'll never know which was which because the goal wasn't to learn *who prefers what*. The goal was to crown one winner and serve it to everyone next time.

The mantra of "always be testing" gives us the illusion of progress, but it's only ever optimizing for a one-size-fits-all approach.

The Workflow of Sameness

Here's how most campaigns are built:

1. Pick the theme.
2. Craft the appeal.
3. Build a list of people to send it to.

The donor is an afterthought, only entering the frame when the system asks, "Whom do I send this to?" And even then, it's binary. Donor A is in; Donor B is out. The system isn't built to instead ask, "What does Donor A need to see and feel to say yes—and how does that differ from Donor B?"

This is the paradox: lots of segmentation talk, but the system is designed for sorting—active, lapsed, midlevel, monthly. These are bookkeeping categories, not windows into motivation that would warrant different treatment. This leaves the fundraiser stuck with when someone last gave and how much, instead of *why* they gave.

The Window Dressing of Personalization

Then those bookkeeping categories get dressed up with small cosmetic tweaks. Swap a line in the copy for "midlevel." Put major donors on nicer paper stock and add a stamp to the reply envelope.

Inside the shop, it feels like tailoring, but to the donor, it's the same letter.

This is why most "segmentation" delivers so little — personalization in name only, a costume over sameness.

The Path Forward

The only way to break free is to understand your donors as people: who they are, what they value, how they're wired. Sorting transactions won't get you there. Swapping a line won't get you there. Optimization without relevance won't get you there.

Part II will show how to do exactly that—how to personalize based on identity, values, and traits, without gimmicks, guesswork, or pretending every donor is an interchangeable wallet.

But first, Chapter 3 looks at why these quick fixes have become fundraising's dominant defaults and why each use makes the underlying problem harder to solve.

Chapter 3
The Non-Fix Fix: Gimmicks, Gifts, and Faux Urgency

And when the volume machine of sameness produces sagging results, it triggers a systemwide scramble for quick fixes and whatever promises an immediate lift: a matching-gift deadline, a premium offer, a flash of manufactured urgency.

What's left is a donor feeling like they've been sold something instead of invited into something.

And the more you use gimmicks and gifts, the more your mission gets crowded out. The message becomes about the tote bag, the deadline, the offer—anything except why your work matters.

You can see it in the conservation appeal in Figure 3.1, which uses soft pleas and free gifts. The polar bear, the actual mission, is relegated to a gratuitous backdrop for a transaction. The merchandise is bigger and bolder than any conservation message. The urgency is artificial. The entire package feels like a limited-time deal, not an invitation to protect something real.

Figure 3.1: Conservation Appeal Using Premium Gimmicks

And this isn't rare. In acquisition mail, 88 percent of packages now rely on premiums, matching gifts, or both. It's become the default approach, not the exception. That feels like we've lost the plot.

The Hidden Costs of Extrinsic Rewards

Behavioral science has long documented that external rewards can undermine intrinsic motivation. In one classic study, children who loved drawing were given rewards for their art. Later, when no prizes were offered, they drew less and reported less enjoyment (Lepper et al. 1973). The reward didn't amplify motivation; it replaced it.

The same dynamic shows up in workplaces. Employees offered bonuses purely tied to output often see their intrinsic motivation decline. The work becomes a transaction. The sense of purpose erodes (Deci et al. 1999).

Fundraising is no different. When you offer a gift as a primary reason to give, you undermine any mission connection. The recipients' decision calculus shifts to the tchotchkes and the external reward. And the double-negative outcome is attracting an audience with no mission connection to begin with.

The Coupon Effect

Matching gifts were once seen as the pinnacle of urgency. Double your impact. Act before the deadline. But research shows that matching offers often act like coupons. They create a discount mindset: "If I act now, I get a deal."

One meta-analysis (Eckel and Grossman 2003) found that while matches can increase the initial response, they rarely increase giving beyond the match period. The urgency evaporates, and so does the donor's connection to your cause. You might call this *defining success downward*: mistaking a temporary spike for sustainable growth.

Why It Persists

So why does the cycle keep repeating? Because these tactics are easy to measure, and campaign reports look like evidence of progress. And they feel safe because everyone else is using them.

But if your only playbook is copying what everyone else is sending and just mailing more of it, then you're mistaking the method, fundraising, for the goal, growth.

There's Another Way

People don't wake up craving another tote bag or matching-gift coupon. They wake up with a sense of self, a set of values, and intrinsic motivations you can understand and speak to. They wake up willing to consider taking action if you give them a reason that feels personal and genuine.

Part II will show how to stop living on the surface and start building the kind of relevance no gimmick can replicate. But these gimmicks persist because the measurement system rewards them and Chapter 4 pulls back the lens on that system.

Chapter 4
Funnel Vision

Gimmicks aren't just harmless shortcuts. They reinforce fundraising's tunnel-vision obsession with short-term results at the expense of long-term growth.

There are two jobs in fundraising, harvesting and planting:

- Harvesting is a direct response. You're picking the crops that are ready right now—sending appeals, retargeting donors, driving immediate gifts.
- Planting is brand building. You're sowing seeds of awareness, trust, and mental availability—so more people will care enough to give tomorrow.

Digital Spend Allocation

Direct Fundraising	**72%**	**Harvest**
Lead Gen	**10%**	**Harvest**
Awareness	14%	Plow
Advocacy	2%	Plow
Other	2%	Plow

Figure 4.1. Most digital spend is on short-term

Both are necessary. If you only plant, you won't have revenue this quarter. But if you only harvest, you eventually run out of field.

Yet most nonprofits spend 90 percent (Figure 4.1) or more of their budgets on harvesting. Why? Partly mindset, partly measurement.

Almost every metric focuses on short-term efficiency, which requires linking immediate spending to immediate revenue. If this month's report doesn't show a return on ad spend (ROAS), brand investment looks like a failure.

So instead of planting, we optimize the harvest.

Attribution Theater

That same fixation on immediacy creates another problem: attribution theater.

Picture this: A midsize nonprofit spends $783,000 across channels and raises $3.1 million. Seems clear enough. But here's where it gets messy:

Your ROAS Reality Check

Channel	Spend	Actual Revenue	Platform-Claimed Revenue	Platform-Reported ROAS	Actual ROAS
Facebook	$125K	$275K	$625K	5:1	2.2:1
Google Search	$100K	$310K	$600K	6:1	3.1:1
Programmatic	$75K	$135K	$225K	3:1	1.8:1
Email	$108K	$1.296M	$4.32M	40:1	12:1
Direct Mail	$375K	$1.084M	$1.5M	4:1	2.7:1
TOTAL	$783K	$3.1M	$7.27M	--	--

Figure 4.2. Channels overclaim revenue

Each channel's report shows the same dollars claimed multiple times (Figure 4.2). Direct mail attributes revenue through matchback analysis. Facebook takes credit through view-through conversions. Email calls it last-touch; paid search claims last-click.

When you add it up, the platforms collectively claim $7.2 million, more than double reality.

It's like every player on a basketball team insisting they scored all 100 points because they touched the ball at some point.

This isn't just a reporting nuisance; it warps budgets. If every channel claims it's the engine of growth, no one wants to cut spending. The result is more money poured into harvesting the same donors repeatedly, whereas planting gets starved.

ROAS Addiction

What gets measured gets managed, and nothing is fetishized more than ROAS.

A shiny 4:1 ROAS feels like proof of effectiveness. But ROAS is just an efficiency metric. It tells you how well you converted existing demand, not whether you created any new demand.

That's why you get the following results:

- Paid search looks like a miracle (8:1 ROAS—you're paying Google to intercept people already searching for you).
- Meta retargeting shows 6:1 returns because you're chasing your own donors across the internet.
- Display ads boast 5:1 returns by hounding people who were likely to give anyway.

You can't retarget your way to transformational growth. At some point, the field is picked clean.

Metrics That Shrink Your Future

One of the largest studies of marketing effectiveness, *The Long and Short of It* by Les Binet and Peter Field (2013), showed that long-term campaigns aimed at planting—building brand salience—always create short-term effects too. But the reverse isn't true: Short-term harvesting campaigns rarely deliver any long-term growth.

As Peter Drucker wrote in *Post-Capitalist Society* (1993), "Long-term results cannot be achieved by piling short-term results on short-term results."

The Cost

When the numbers inevitably slip, the reflex is always the same: more volume, more sameness, more gimmicks.

Over time, this doesn't just exhaust your donors. It rewires how they see you.

It's the final stage of the cycle, scrambling for marginal gains in a field you've already picked clean.

That's the complete picture of the volume machine: a system that asks too much, says the same thing to everyone, reaches for shortcuts when it stalls, and measures only what it can claim immediate credit for. Each flaw feeds the others.

Breaking the cycle requires building something structurally different, a fundraising system designed around the donor as a person, not a transaction record.

Part II: Personalization—Harvesting Today's Demand the Right Way

Chapter 5
The Necessary Ingredients

Motivation Type Behind the Giving	How People Feel on Inside	Correlation with Life-Time Value
Personal connection	**Giving to brand is personally meaningful to me**	Positive
Warm glow	Giving to brand makes me proud	Negative
Guilt induced	I would feel bad about myself if I didn't give to brand	Negative
Social pressure	I feel pressured by others to give to brand	Negative
Lighting-in-bottle giving	I don't have a good reason for why I gave to brand	Negative

Figure 5.1. The only sticky giving is autobiographical

Donors don't keep giving because they were asked often or cleverly. They keep giving when the act means something to them. Psychologists call this *intrinsic motivation*. You might call it *personal connection*. Both refer to the same thing: giving driven by internal values rather than pressure, guilt, or fleeting emotion.

And the data make the distinction painfully clear (Figure 5.1).

The donors with high-quality, intrinsic motivation keep going. The donors with low-quality motivation –guilt, obligation, or momentary warm glow—fall away quickly. Warm glow is pleasant, but it evaporates fast and doesn't anchor the relationship, and guilt burns out even faster.

Meaning is what holds.

Self-Determination Theory is clear on what produces that meaning; it requires three psychological needs that underlie all high-quality motivation—autonomy, competence, and relatedness. They aren't abstractions. They are the donor's felt experience that giving is my choice, a smart choice, and a choice that connects to who I am.

- **Relatedness:** The donor feels emotionally connected to the people or situation.
- **Competence:** The donor believes their action will work.
- **Autonomy:** The donor feels free, not pressured, in choosing to act.

When a message aligns with how a donor sees the world, all three needs reinforce one another. The donor feels recognized (relatedness), the decision feels self-expressive rather than externally pushed (autonomy), and the choice feels rational and effective (competence). That is the engine of high-quality motivation driving higher lifetime value.

The only way to pull this off is by matching the message to the person. We use four interconnected elements:

- **Identity:** their connection to the mission
- **Personality:** how they process the world
- **Moral Frame:** their moral lens of right/wrong
- **Emotion:** what we want them to feel

Pillar 1: Personalization with depth

The design question shifts from "Whom do we send this to?" to "What does this person need to see and feel for a yes to be natural?"

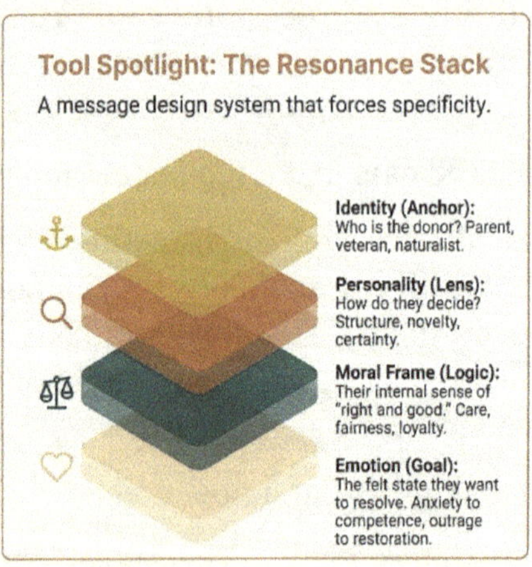

Figure 5.2. An applied model to deliver real personalization

These aren't separate concepts; they form a stack called the *resonance stack (*Figure 5.2). Personality follows identity and, in turn, informs moral framing. Those moral intuitions steer which emotional palette feels natural and believable. These linkages are well established in behavioral science and give you a structure you can apply at scale without reducing donors to caricatures.

This is the opposite of choice paralysis. With a structured stack, the choices narrow. You're painting by numbers, but the result is a custom portrait. The constraints liberate you because they force you to write to *someone*, not *everyone.*

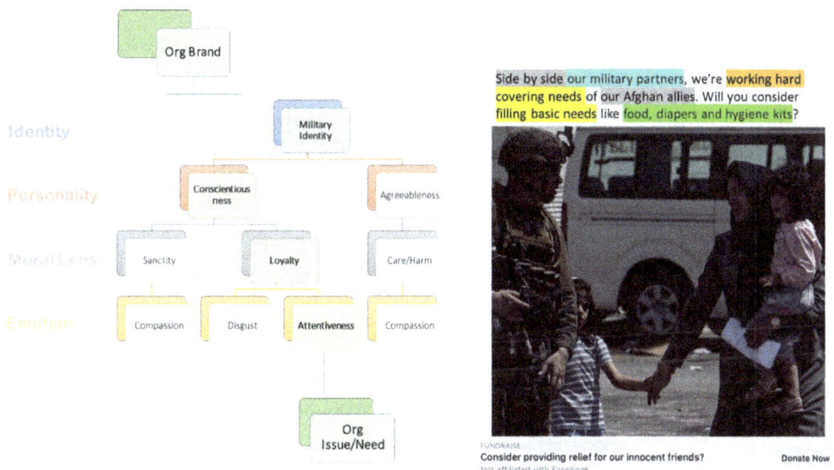

Figure 5.3. How Match Message to Who Donor Is

An example: This ad (Figure 5.3) was designed for a charity and uses the resonance stack with a military-connected mission. Every word of note in this ad was purposeful, chosen to speak to this specific person. The highlighted colors show the choices and the coordination.

Blue: The phrase "our military partners" speaks to the reader's shared *Identity* of a direct military connection.

Orange: The phrase "working hard" targets those high in conscientiousness because these are people who value hard work.

Gray: The phrases "side by side" and "our Afghan allies" invoke a moral choice about supporting those to whom we're loyal.

Yellow: The phrases "covering needs" and "filling basic needs" show attentiveness to a person's needs and how this loyal, conscientious military person often expresses themselves emotionally.

Green: The phrase "food, diapers and hygiene kit" helps satisfy a sense of accomplishment with a tangible good.

Identity: The Anchor of Meaning

Age, income, gender, generation, political affiliation—we can easily and quickly sort people based on these qualities. And if asked, each person can sort themselves into these categories, which means every person carries multiple identities at once.

You can be a parent, an activist, a volunteer, a caregiver, a veteran, and a donor. But having an identity is not the same as acting from it. What drives behavior is not whether someone belongs to an identity category but whether that identity is active in the moment of decision.

Identities are hierarchical and situational. Each one carries a set of values, goals, and norms about how someone with that identity behaves. Which identity guides behavior depends on which one the situation makes salient. When an identity is activated, we do not deliberate from scratch; we instinctively evaluate choices to see whether taking the action is in keeping with that identity. It makes decision making easier because we don't have to overthink it; we simply react instinctively.

A well-documented example comes from research on policing. In the United States, police officers skew heavily White and Republican. Republicans, on average, express stronger support for aggressive policing than Democrats. You might expect those personal identities to show up in enforcement behavior.

They do not.

Across large administrative data sets examining arrests, stops, and use of force, researchers find no meaningful differences by race or political affiliation once officers are on duty. A White Republican officer and a Black Democratic officer behave the same way in comparable situations.

The reason is not that personal identity disappears; it is that it's overridden. When officers put on the uniform and step into their role, the dominant identity becomes that of police officer. That identity comes bundled with training, norms, expectations, and a shared sense of purpose. Once activated, it swamps everything else.

This is how identity works for all of us. We do not consciously choose which identity to act from. Context does that for us—for example, seeing a charity appeal. And when the right identity is active, behavior aligns with its values almost automatically.

Mission–Identity Fit: The Identity That Drives Action

The identity that reliably drives giving is the one that fits the mission.

We call this *Mission –Identity Fit*. It is the alignment between how a donor sees themselves in this context and the core purpose of the organization.

- This is why caregivers donate to disease-related charities connected to their experience.
- This is why conservationists support environmental organizations.
- This is why veterans give to veterans' groups.
- This is why people with a strong community identity support local causes.

In each case, the donor is not responding as a demographic. They are responding as a version of themselves for whom the mission is personally meaningful. Supporting the organization feels consistent with who they are and what they value.

When there is a strong mission–identity fit, then saying yes reinforces the donor's self-concept and affirms values they already hold and the goals they already care about. Little persuasion is required because the choice already makes sense.

A donor can give without identity fit, but those gifts are fragile and often require external reasons to give—a premium, a matching-gift offer. These folks may convert today, but they are much more likely to disappear tomorrow.

Identity Activation and the Job of Messaging

The job of fundraising messaging is not persuasion in the traditional sense; it is activation.

Effective messaging makes a mission-relevant identity salient at the moment of decision and makes it easy for the donor to see how supporting the organization is consistent with the values and goals attached to that identity. When this happens, the donor is not asking, Should I give? They are asking, what would someone like me do?

Knowing who your donors are is not the same as activating who they are. You can have caregivers in your file and still write messages that never call that identity forward. You can tell stories without making it clear how giving expresses the donor's sense of self.

When identity is activated, giving shifts from transactional to self-expressive. It stops feeling like a response to a request and starts feeling like an affirmation of who the donor is.

Get mission–identity fit right, and fundraising becomes easier and more durable. Get it wrong, and every other lever must work harder, more often, and with diminishing returns.

How to Discover the Identities That Matter

1. **Form hypotheses.**
    - Ask yourself what type of person might be attracted to your cause. List those that plausibly relate to your mission.
    - This is not "people who care about [issue]" (e.g., medical research, voting rights, conserving open space).

- These aren't labels that require your organization to be in the mix (e.g., member, alumni, donor).
- These are self-labels that exist independently of your organization (e.g., caregiver, conservationist, activist, veteran, dog lover).

2. **Validate the identities.**
   - **Step 1:** Write survey questions that surface those identities. Identity is revealed through *self-labeling*, not inference. Ask donors which role describes them, which statements feel like them, and which motivations they resonate with. There are plenty of existing survey items in the public domain; a query with your favorite large language model (LLM; e.g., ChatGPT) to research and develop these survey items is your cheapest, best route.
   - **Step 2:** Once you've collected identity data in a survey, you need to determine which identities organize behavior. Look at the identity groups and their giving patterns, response rates, retention, and upgrade behavior. A real identity isn't just psychologically plausible; it also shows up in the numbers. This means you'll see differences in behavior between those who have a certain identity (e.g., conservationist) and those who do not. That is the moment you know you have something causal, not coincidental.

The survey questions used to identify the validated identities are your zero-party "magic questions." Your opportunity and imperative is to ask these questions in as many places as possible and, ideally, as early in the relationship as possible, for example, as part of the new donor acquisition or welcome process.

Such **zero-party data**, which are willingly shared by supporters, constitute a data asset that is unique to you. Record these data on the supporter's constituent record in the same way you would their contact details. These data tell you why they support your cause, making them as valuable as the supporter's bank details because they reveal what message, offers, and calls to action will spring them to action.

One medical charity asks supporters their connection to pediatric cancer, and in a mere eighteen months, this charity had gathered zero-party data for over six hundred thousand donors by making it an organizational imperative. The charity asked the magic questions in preexisting communications; in post interaction feedback surveys; and as stand-alone, new touchpoints.

Using Third-Party Data as a Head Start

Third-party data can accelerate this work. It can serve as a proxy to start tagging your file with initial identity data. This creates a two-tier system: Third-party data = head start. Zero-party data = truth.

And combining them gives you identity coverage across a far larger portion of your file than surveys alone.

A hospital specializing in LGBTQ care conducted primary research that revealed two distinct identities within the hospital's donor file:

- **HIV Legacy Supporter.** This is a gay man who lived through the AIDS epidemic, and his association with the organization dates from that period.
- **Community Supporter.** This person is very committed to the figurative LGBTQ community but also to the physical community where the hospital is located.

Third-party data were used as a proxy to score the donor file with these two identities.

The two postcard mailers (Figure 5.4) were crafted to match the respective identities; they weren't sent as a head-to-head contest to find the winner, and they were matched to the audience. And each outperformed the control, also sent to each audience, by an average of 7 percent in terms of conversion.

Identity Case Study: Health Care Appeal

Response Rate Increased by 7%

Average Gift Increased by 78%

Figure 5.4. Matching Message and Creative to Identity

Identity determines whether someone is even a good prospect for your mission. It explains why your work could matter to them at all. Personality, moral frame, and emotion do not create that fit; they shape how a relevant message should be expressed once the fit exists.

You cannot manufacture mission–identity fit. It already exists, or it does not. Your best supporters are those for whom your mission aligns with how they see themselves in this context. That alignment defines your real target market, not demographics or transaction history.

The job of messaging is to make that fit explicit. Every signal you send should help the right people recognize themselves and help everyone else quietly opt out. When identity fit is clear, giving feels natural and self-expressive. When it is vague or hidden, fundraising must rely on pressure and tactics to compensate.

Everything else flows from mission–identity fit.

Personality: The Trait Layer That Shapes How Identity Shows Up

Identity tells you *why* a donor might care about your cause. Personality tells you *how* that identity expresses itself. Two people can share the same identity—parent, veteran, caregiver, naturalist—and behave in entirely different ways because they differ in their underlying trait profiles. This is why personality sits directly beneath identity in the resonance stack. It adds texture, variation, and precision.

The framework we use is the **Big Five**, the most empirically validated model of personality in the behavioral sciences. It predates the Myers–Briggs Type Indicator (MBTI), has deeper psychometric backing, and is far more predictive of real-world behavior. But it never had the marketing machine that turned MBTI into a corporate horoscope, so it remains underrecognized outside academic circles. Big Five has substance, but it lacks a public relations (PR) agent.

According to the Big Five, our personality can be described by our scores on five traits: openness, conscientiousness, extraversion, agreeableness, and neuroticism, also referred to by their acronym, OCEAN. Here's what each of the traits means:

Openness to Experience: A tendency toward curiosity, imagination, ideas, creativity, and exploration.

How it shows up in fundraising: These donors try new things. They explore. They notice nuance. They respond to metaphor, narrative, and conceptual framing. They are drawn to missions that expand understanding, possibility, or human potential. They are comfortable with ambiguity and complexity.

What it predicts in message relevance:

- Rich, sensory storytelling
- Broader meaning and values-based arguments
- Novel framing or unexpected angles
- Emotional language that conveys depth rather than urgency
- Future orientation ("What could be possible if . . .")

What to avoid:

- Clichés, rigid formulas, simplistic binaries, dry appeals, overt transactional framing

Openness donors respond when you let the mission breathe, when you give them an idea or a story that expands their understanding of the world and lets them imagine a better version of it.

Conscientiousness: Organization, discipline, structure, reliability, goal-directed behavior.

How it shows up in fundraising: These donors follow routines. They keep commitments. They value order. They respond to earn-and-deserve logic. They want clarity, specificity, and predictable follow-through. They show up in your retention numbers because they stick with things they believe in.

What it predicts in message relevance:

- Duty, responsibility, commitment
- Structure ("here's the plan," "step by step")
- Tangible outputs and reliable execution
- Messages that highlight stability, safety, and accountability
- Language that affirms identity as responsible or dependable

What to avoid:

- Loose narratives, ambiguous asks, emotional chaos, overpromising without proof

Conscientious donors want to feel they are doing the right thing the right way—and that you are too.

Extraversion: Sociability, energy, enthusiasm, a preference for interpersonal engagement.

How it shows up in fundraising: These donors lean into group settings, shared action, collaboration, and collective momentum. They gravitate toward visible participation, community experiences, events, volunteerism, and social proof.

What it predicts in message relevance:

- "Join us," "stand with us," "together we can . . ."
- Collective identity ("people like us make things happen")
- Social validation ("thousands of supporters stepped up")
- High-energy emotional tone
- Opportunities for public or semipublic participation

What to avoid:

- Appeals framed as solitary reflection, overly quiet emotional registers, isolating or self-contained narratives

Extraverts want connection and movement. They respond to missions that feel alive, communal, and socially charged.

Agreeableness: Compassion, warmth, trust, cooperativeness, and emotional attunement.

How it shows up in fundraising: These donors prioritize harmony and care. They avoid conflict. They want to help people. They gravitate to causes where the emotional core is nurturing, healing, comforting, or protecting.

What it predicts in message relevance:

- Gentle, compassionate language
- Human-centered storytelling
- Moral framing around care and fairness
- "You can help someone today" language
- Messages that emphasize connection and empathy

What to avoid:

- Confrontational tone, harshness, aggressive urgency, cynicism, anything that feels cold or transactional.

Agreeable donors give when the appeal feels warm, relational, and emotionally safe—when helping feels like the natural thing to do.

Neuroticism (Emotional Stability): Neuroticism reflects sensitivity to threat, stress, uncertainty, and potential negative outcomes. Emotional stability is the inverse—calm under pressure, steady affect, and low reactivity to stress.

How it shows up in fundraising: These individuals scan for potential downside and want reassurance. They look for signals of control, predictability, and reduced uncertainty.

What it predicts in message relevance:

- Clear reassurance
- Emphasis on protection, safeguarding, and harm prevention
- Emotional tone that acknowledges concern but resolves it
- Messages that provide relief ("you can prevent or reduce the chance of X happening")

What to avoid:

- Ambiguity or lack of clarity
- Unresolved risk or open loops
- Fear without a clear path to resolution

Every person has a score on all five traits, but for most people, one or two are dominant traits. Those dominant traits steer what captures attention, what feels credible, what feels motivating, and what feels off. Trait dominance shapes what we notice, what we ignore, and how we decide.

This isn't speculation. Decades of research (Roberts et al. 2007) show how trait profiles correlate with choices, both big and small. Take almost any human domain—political persuasion, consumer behavior, musical preference, pet ownership, where you live, career choice, risk taking, health habits, charitable giving—and trait dominance quietly, consistently predicts outcomes.

The Big Five model has become the backbone of modern psychological prediction for a reason: it works.

For fundraisers, the point is straightforward: Not all people within the same identity respond to the same message. Two veterans aren't the same, two parents aren't the same, and two environmentalists aren't the same.

Ignoring trait variation is how you flatten relevance and slide back into the beige middle of messaging.

How We Score Traits Without Administering a Personality Test

Unlike identity, which requires self-labeling and weaker signals in third-party data, trait dominance can be inferred. The code has been cracked; there is a commercially available data product (i.e., Personality Tags™ from DonorVoice) to append scores for all five traits to your donor file without administering a single survey question.

Here's how it works.

Third-party data provide hundreds of behavioral signals—financial habits, media choices, hobbies, purchasing categories, organizational memberships, household structure, voting patterns, content preferences, and so forth. None of these signals, individually, *is* personality. But each reflects micro-choices shaped by personality.

Think of these data points as raw ingredients and the scoring models as recipes—formulas that determine which ingredients predict which trait, and in what proportions.

For example, conscientious people are more likely to drive trucks, shop at big-box stores, own a dog, and drink domestic beer. These are correlations, not stereotypes, and the underlying pattern is a preference for structure, familiarity, and order.

Those high in openness are more likely to travel internationally, be highly educated, and enjoy fine wine and cultural events. Again, the pattern is the point: curiosity, exploration, and aesthetic complexity.

The model takes hundreds of ingredients and combines them into a stable, predictive trait score for each individual. The result is trait coverage across your entire file. And once you have these scores, there is no need to re-tag the names as traits are stable over time.

Why Tailoring to Trait Matters

Trait is the design layer that determines which version of your message resonates with which person. If identity is the role the donor brings to the relationship, then trait is the style in which they inhabit that role.

- A conscientious veteran responds to duty, reliability, structured support, and fulfilling a commitment.
- An open veteran responds to values, curiosity, and the human story behind the mission.
- An agreeable veteran responds to care, compassion, and protecting those in harm's way.
- An extroverted veteran responds to community, camaraderie, and acting together.
- A neurotic veteran responds to risk, uncertainty, reassurance, and reducing the chance of things going wrong.

So, with the same identity—veteran—there are five different trait-driven openings, five different emotional routes into the ask.

A Case Study: Figure 5.5 shows the opening sentence for five different, accurate renditions of the story of a woman, Isabella, who lived in near darkness for decades with cataracts in both eyes. Each version is purpose built to match a specific trait. The tailoring resulted in a 21 percent increase in response rate compared with the one-size-fits-all control.

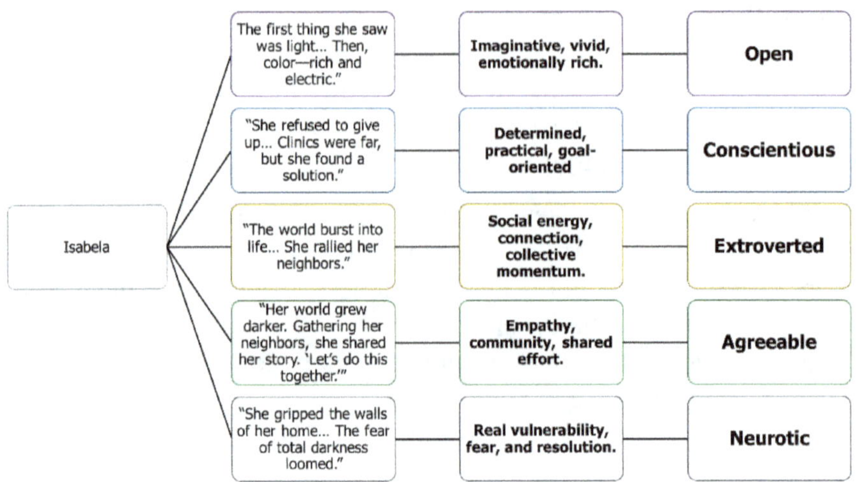

Figure 5.5. Same story, framed differently to match reader.

A Case Study: Figure 5.6 shows a test for those scoring high in openness, based on Personality Tags™ purchased by the organization. These high-openness supporters were randomly assigned to receive either the control creative (shown on the left) or the test creative (shown on the right). No other supporters were included in this comparison. The uplift shown is not an average effect across the file. It is a segment-specific effect by design.

The control represents a standard one-size-fits-all approach. The test creative was intentionally designed to align with what decades of personality research tell us about people high in openness: They are more drawn to novelty, aesthetic richness, abstraction, imagination, and experiences that feel expansive rather than prescriptive.

Figure 5.6. Message matched to person versus one size fits all.

Image Strategy

The control image depicts a familiar, literal scene: a child in a park. It is grounded, concrete, and emotionally safe. This type of imagery performs adequately with broad audiences because it is easy to process and emotionally unambiguous. It asks very little of the viewer and leaves little room for interpretation.

The test image makes a fundamentally different demand. It centers on sculpture rather than people, motion rather than stillness, and symbolism rather than literal representation. The statue is midleap, arms extended, surrounded by light and texture. Meaning is implied rather than explained.

For high-openness individuals, this ambiguity isn't friction; these supporters are more comfortable with open-ended interpretation and more likely to find meaning through metaphor than instruction. The image does not tell them what to feel; it allows them to project meaning, complete the story, and emotionally enter the scene themselves.

Copy Strategy

The copy follows the same logic. The control copy is informational and functional. It explains what the park is, why it matters, and what action to take. It is clear, but it is also bounded. The reader is treated as someone who needs to be persuaded through explanation and reminders.

The test copy shifts from explanation to evocation. Rather than leading with programs or outcomes, it opens with a question about beauty, wonder, and experience. The language is intentionally more abstract and experiential. Phrases such as "a sense of wonder" and "the beauty and magic of our Park" are nonspecific by design. They activate internal imagery rather than external instruction.

This approach is not accidental. High-openness individuals respond more strongly to language that connects to curiosity, imagination, and self-concept. The copy does not narrow attention to a single problem or program. It broadens the mental aperture and allows the donor to locate themselves emotionally within the mission. Even the call to action is framed less as an obligation and more as participation in something meaningful and expansive.

What the Result Tells Us

The 1,460 percent increase in ROI is not evidence that this creative is universally better; it isn't. It is evidence that fit matters.

When image and language align with how a person naturally processes meaning, the decision to give feels easier. The supporter is not being convinced to give; they're being reminded why this kind of place and this kind of experience matter to them.

This exposes the core failure of one-size-fits-all fundraising: It assumes the same creative should work equally well across different psychological profiles. This test shows the opposite. The same organization, the same ask, and the same channel produce radically different outcomes depending on whether the message speaks the donor's language.

The implication is unavoidable: Relevance cannot be manufactured through better copy alone. It emerges when you stop talking to donors as an abstract group and start designing for real differences in how people see, feel, and interpret the world.

Why This Test Matters

In a traditional split test, recipients are randomized, and each version is sent to half the file. In our current example, the child-at-the-fountain image would likely "win," and the result would be logged as best practice.

But that kind of testing rests on a faulty assumption: that all donors are fundamentally the same. When you randomize everyone, the spreadsheet produces one clean average. Inside that average are people who responded strongly and people who rejected the message entirely. Their reactions cancel each other out.

This happens in nearly every "random *n*th" test in the sector. Ideas do not fail as often as people-level differences get averaged away. The real signal is not the mean; it's the variance, those who liked the test and those who didn't. It's the psychological pattern hiding inside the data.

In this test, we removed the randomness of who receives what. The openness-tailored creative was matched only to donors high in openness. Instead of asking, "Which creative wins overall?", the test asks a more precise question: "Which creative works for this type of person?"

This is not creative optimization; it is behavioral design. And it is how you stop forcing donors into an average and start designing for who they are.

Moral Frame: The Donor's Internal Logic of "Right and Good"

Most charitable asks are moral choices, asking the donor to decide what's right, what's fair, what deserves protection, who deserves help, and what kind of person they want to be in that moment.

Most appeals ignore this and default to generic moral language of "make a difference," "help someone today," or "it's the right thing to do." But beneath the surface, donors use moral intuitions to judge your request, not consciously but automatically and instinctively.

This is where **moral foundations theory** (MFT) becomes indispensable.

MFT proposes several core moral "taste buds" people draw on when interpreting what is right or wrong. They are as follows:

- **Care/Harm -:** Sensitivity to suffering and compassion for others versus cruelty
- **Fairness/Cheating -:** Concern for proportionality, reciprocity, and justice versus exploitation
- **Loyalty/Betrayal -:** Valuing group cohesion and standing by your team versus disloyalty
- **Authority/Subversion -:** Respect for hierarchy, tradition, and legitimate leadership versus rebellion
- **Sanctity/Degradation -:** Sense of purity, sacredness, and elevation versus contamination or disgust

Different people emphasize different foundations, depending on their personality, upbringing, worldview, and identity. That variation is why one donor responds strongly to a message about protecting vulnerable children (care orientation) while another responds to honoring a commitment to veterans (loyalty + authority orientation).

If your fundraising messages unconsciously lean on providing care or preventing harm, they will only fit a subset of donors. This is the opportunity: Use trait dominance to guide which moral frame fits which donor.

How to Message for Each Moral Foundation with Trait Pairings

There are clear correlations between trait dominance and moral intuition, but the point is not that personality *determines* morality; it's that it tilts it. Trait gives you the most probable moral frame a donor will use when evaluating your request.

This is why we place moral frame *after* trait in the resonance stack:

1. Identity tells you what they care about.
2. Trait tells you how they think and make decisions.
3. Moral frame tells you *why* the message feels right, wrong, or worth acting on.

Here is how each moral foundation can be messaged and how trait changes the tone or angle:

1. Care/Harm

Moral logic: Protect the vulnerable. Reduce suffering.

Trait match: High agreeableness, high openness, high neuroticism (especially the reduce-harm angle)

Messaging angle:

- "Your kindness keeps a child safe tonight."
- "No one should face this alone."
- "Your compassion prevents real harm."

Tone: Warm, nurturing, emotionally attuned

Avoid: Harshness, confrontation, aggressive urgency

2. Fairness/Cheating

Moral logic: Everyone deserves a fair chance. Justice should be upheld.

Trait match: High openness, high agreeableness

Messaging angle:

- "Everyone deserves the same shot at safety."
- "This is about fairness, not charity."
- "You can correct an injustice today."

Tone: Values-driven, principled, sometimes idealistic

Avoid: Provincial language and narrow group appeals

3. Loyalty/Betrayal

Moral logic: Stand with your people. Honor those who've earned allegiance.

Trait match: High conscientiousness, high extraversion

Messaging angle:

- "We take care of our own."
- "They stood for us—now we stand for them."
- "Honor the commitment. Don't leave them behind."

Tone: Proud, steadfast, communal

Avoid: Hyperemotionality, which dilutes the moral seriousness

4. Authority/Subversion

Moral logic: Respect the structure that keeps order.

Trait match: High conscientiousness, low neuroticism

Messaging angle:

- "This is the responsible action."
- "Follow through on the values we were taught."
- "Strong leadership. Clear results. Your gift strengthens the backbone of this mission."

Tone: Disciplined, confident, orderly

Avoid: Informality or anything that feels improvisational

5. Sanctity/Degradation

Moral logic: Protect what is pure, sacred, or worthy of reverence.

Trait match: High agreeableness, high conscientiousness (depending on context)

Messaging angle:

- "Preserve what should never be lost."
- "This is about dignity."
- "Some things must be protected."

Tone: Reverent, elevated, sometimes symbolic

Avoid: Graphic content or anything that feels flippant

Why Using Trait to Choose a Moral Frame Matters

There is no perfect or predetermined mapping, and you don't need one. Trait doesn't eliminate creative choice; it provides guardrails.

Without trait, you're choosing moral frames in the dark, and with trait, the choices narrow to what is psychologically plausible, moving from infinite options to a defined set that will make sense to the recipient.

That's the entire point of the resonance stack: constraint as clarity.

- A veteran high in conscientiousness might respond to this appeal: "We honor the commitment. Duty carried through."
- A veteran high in openness might respond to this appeal: "Their story deserves to be known and carried forward."

Same identity, two personality types, two moral frames, two emotional worlds, two outcomes, each optimized to the person versus against each other. This is how you escape the sea of sameness.

Emotion: The Goal, Not the Cause

Emotion sits last in the resonance stack for a reason: It's the surface expression of everything underneath it—identity, trait, and moral frame. You don't start with emotion; you end with it. You choose the emotional path only after you know whom you are speaking to, how they interpret the world, and what moral logic they use to judge what is right.

A lot of "best-practice" guidance inverts this, jumping to sadness or anger and hoping the rest follows. That is why the sector has leaned so heavily on generic sadness for decades and why performance and retention have stagnated.

This stems from perhaps the most pervasive, subtle, but critical misunderstanding in fundraising: Emotion is not the cause of giving; it's the *goal state* donors seek through giving.

People act when they believe their action will change how they feel. They do not give because you made them sad; they give because they believe giving will relieve sadness, mollify their anger, foster a sense of hope, and so forth.

This distinction is fundamental. Without it, everything else becomes emotional noise.

Emotion Motivates Only When There Is a Path to Relief

Robert Cialdini's mood-freeze experiments (Manucia et al. 1984) make this point unmistakable.

Researchers put one group of participants into a sad mood and left another neutral by asking the groups to read a distressing paragraph and a neutral one, respectively. Then they split each mood group into two. Half received a placebo described as a "mood-freezing drug," supposedly locking their mood in place for an hour. These participants had the impression that their current mood (sad or neutral) would stay fixed no matter what they did in the next hour. The other half wasn't given a pill and therefore assumed their mood could change. Then all participants were given the chance to help someone.

Only one group reliably helped: the sad participants who believed their mood could change.

The sad participants who believed their mood was frozen were the *least* likely to help.

If sadness *caused* helping, both sad groups should have acted. Instead, behavior shifted based on the anticipated emotional outcome: whether helping would make them feel better.

This is the psychological mechanism fundraising must respect: **Negative emotion motivates action only when the donor can see that giving will resolve or improve that emotion.**

What drives giving is not the emotion you feel in the moment but the emotion you expect to feel afterward, your anticipated emotion. People imagine how they will feel if they act and decide based on that expectation. Will I feel relief? Will I feel like I helped? Will I feel like I did the right thing?

This is why making people sad or angry is not enough. Those emotions only matter if giving is clearly positioned as the way to resolve them. The decision is guided by anticipated relief and emotional payoff, not by distress itself.

So, yes, you can use sadness or anger, but only as the first half of a two-part design: tension, then resolution.

Creating that tension differs by emotion types, which follow different cognitive rules.

Low-certainty emotions, such as sadness and worry, create uncertainty about what is going to happen next. It's akin to standing in a dimly lit room: You can see the outline of what's happening, but the details aren't all filled in. As a result, you start paying more attention, and your mind naturally tries to fill in the blanks.

Low-certainty emotions create more cognitive willingness to keep reading, to stay engaged, because the donor is actively completing the emotional picture, which keeps them open to what comes next.

That internal engagement gives you more room to guide the emotional turn toward a hopeful resolution. With high-certainty emotions, you get no such runway; you must reframe the emotion immediately or lose the donor.

High-certainty emotions, such as disgust or outrage, slam the door quickly with an immediate, definite interpretation of what's happening; your mind snaps to a conclusion instantly.

These emotions tell you exactly what the situation is and what you should feel about it, without requiring any thought. They deliver a verdict. It's like a bright flashlight switched on: Everything is exposed instantly, leaving no room for interpretation.

This creates a *reflex mode*; your brain jumps into action or avoidance. This means donors shut down if you don't immediately give them context or a solution. Without that, they either recoil (disgust) or get overwhelmed (anger). With proper framing, they can become powerful, but only because the action feels clear and achievable.

This distinction explains why the following hold true:

- Sadness-only images often outperform disgust-only images.
- Disgust paired with context can perform just as well as sadness.
- Sadness paired with too much explanation *kills* empathy because it removes ambiguity and forces a cognitive shift.
- Appeals built entirely on anger or fear often backfire unless the donor already sees themselves as an advocate or protector.

Emotion Must Match Trait and Moral Frame

Emotion is not chosen freely. It is chosen from within the donor's psychological structure. Each trait–moral frame combination produces an emotional tone that feels natural to that person:

Agreeableness + Care Frame
Warmth, empathy, gentle sadness, relief

Conscientiousness + Loyalty/Authority Frame
Resolve, duty, responsibility, sober pride

Openness + Fairness/Liberty Frame
Uplift, shared humanity, principled hope

Extraversion + Loyalty Frame
Energy, collective momentum, camaraderie

Emotional Stability + Authority Frame
Calm strength, competence, confidence

This is your emotional palette, a psychologically coherent emotional stance that fits the donor's worldview.

Emotion Lives in Actions, Not Labels

Literal emotion words (e.g., *"sad*, *"angry*, *"happy*) dull the writing. They make the donor observe the story from the outside.

Emotion is evoked through verbs and actions because they trigger lived experience:

- crying
- trembling
- slamming
- whispering
- collapsing
- rising
- gripping
- hesitating
- steadying

These are the cognitive shortcuts that generate emotional resonance. They reduce processing effort and increase immersion. They let the donor *feel* instead of being told *what* to feel.

This matters because emotional engagement is fragile. Every cognitive demand you add—extra explanation, literal labels, abstract adjectives—risks breaking it.

Emotion Must Move

Emotion only works when it moves somewhere. Static despair paralyzes; static positivity bores. The effective pattern is consistent across studies: **Start negative; end hopeful.**

The negative sets the baseline, and the turn creates contrast. The hope becomes believable, and the donor sees their role clearly in producing the resolution.

Research on nearly ten thousand crowdfunding campaigns (Alzaanin 2025) backs this up. Campaigns that begin with real hardship and then move toward resolution raise more than those that linger in despair or skip the struggle altogether. The shape of the story matters.

The story arc works because it matches how people regulate emotion. When a story moves from problem to possibility, the brain responds, and tension activates attention.

The moment of resolution delivers relief, a small dopamine release, and a sense of closure. People are not drawn to sit inside pain, and they are not energized by empty cheerleading. They want movement, the feeling that something broken can be made right.

For that to happen, the donor must mentally complete a simple sequence.

This is wrong → This can be fixed → I can help fix it.

When the story never leaves despair, the brain stays stuck, and the response is withdrawal. When the story skips straight to optimism, the donor is unnecessary. The sweet spot is the moment where resolution is visible but not complete, where the emotional payoff is high and the donor's action is what closes the loop.

Designing Your Resonance Stack—an Exercise Sheet

The point of this stack is not academic; it's a design system, a way to build tailored messages that fit a specific donor, not the average donor.

Here is your prescriptive, repeatable structure.

Step 1: Find the donor's *identity role*

Identity is the anchor. Everything else rests on it.

Ask: What type of person, independent of our organization, would naturally feel connected to this mission?

Examples: Parent, veteran, naturalist, advocate, teacher, global citizen, caregiver

Fill this in:

IDENTITY: "The person who might support our mission sees themselves as a ____________."

Identity determines the following:

- The values that travel with the donor
- The lens through which they understand the mission
- The kinds of stories that feel relevant

Identity = the "hat" you want to call forward in the message.

Step 2: Choose the most plausible dominant *trait style*

Trait shapes how the identity expresses itself.

You are not doing pop psychology. You are choosing the *most probable processing style* for this identity.

Ask: What is the dominant style this person brings to decisions?

Guiding patterns:

- Religious/traditional identities → conscientiousness + agreeableness
- Global/international identities → openness
- Military/service identities → conscientiousness + emotional stability
- Community builders → extraversion or agreeableness
- Analytical roles → emotional stability + openness

Fill this in:

TRAIT: "This identity, in this context, is most likely high in ______________."

Trait determines the following:

- Word choice, the tone, the pacing, the level of detail, the emotional bandwidth

In other words: Trait guides how your message should feel.

Step 3: Select the moral frame the donor will use to judge the appeal

Moral frames determine what counts as "right" or "worth doing."

Ask: Given the identity and trait, which moral foundation will they apply?

Mappings:

- Agreeableness → care
- Openness → fairness (or liberty)
- Conscientiousness → loyalty or authority
- Extraversion → loyalty/group action
- Emotional stability → authority

Fill this in:

MORAL FRAME: "The donor evaluates this request through the lens of _____________."

The moral frame constrains which arguments will resonate and which will fall flat.

Step 4: Choose the emotional stance that naturally flows from that moral frame

Emotion is chosen last, not first.

Ask: If this donor sees the world through this moral frame, what emotion makes that logic feel true?

Derived mapping:

- Care → empathy and protectiveness
- Fairness → principled hope and clarity

- Loyalty → resolve, duty, pride
- Authority → confidence, steadiness, responsibility
- Sanctity → reverence and preservation

Fill this in:

EMOTION: "The emotional stance that fits this frame is ____________."

This becomes the tone of the appeal, not the plot.

Step 5: Translate the stack into message choices

Now you connect the psychological structure to the actual copy.

Ask:

- Identity: Whose story should we tell? What keywords, images, or reference points activate this identity?
- Trait: What writing style matches this processing style? Structured? Warm? Energetic? Values based?
- Moral frame: What moral logic should you cue? Fairness? Care? Loyalty?
- Emotion: What feeling should the donor experience as they move through the story? Duty? Compassion? Curiosity? Hope?

Step 6: Build the narrative arc

Ask: How will the reader/viewer move from tension → possibility → resolution they can enable?

Fill this in:

- Tension: _______________
- Possibility: _______________
- Donor-enabled resolution: _______________

This ensures you don't get stuck in despair or jump straight to premature hope.

Step 7: Choose the verbs (not the emotion words)

Emotion lives in actions.

List the verbs that will express the emotional stance.

Action verbs: _______________

This is where you turn psychology into language.

This is your people-layering system, your way to ask and answer, "What do I send to this person?" instead of "Whom do I send this thing to?"

The resonance stack gives you the ingredients; the next chapter shows you how to build the meal.

Chapter 6
The Anatomy of an Appeal

The prior chapter gave you the people ingredients: identity, trait, moral frame, and emotion. Those tell us whom we're writing to. Now we turn to the second half of the system: how to write in a way the donor's mind can follow, feel, and act on.

Before we get to structure, we need to confront an uncomfortable truth: **The sector doesn't write so well**. We know this not because it "feels true" but because we measured it.

DonorVoice built a tool called **Copy Optimizer**, which analyzes fundraising copy at the linguistic level—parts of speech, tense, pronoun use, verb structure, noun density—and scores writing on two critical dimensions:

1. **Readability:** Does it sound like a personal letter? Is it conversational and easy to understand?
2. **Narrative:** Does it read like a story? Is it immersive and engaging?

We used this tool to analyze two thousand nonprofit appeals from eighty organizations across eight verticals. Here is what we found:

- The average **storytelling score was 28/100**.
- The average **readability score was 50/100**.
- The median overall engagement was **38/100**.

Fundraising copy, on average, reads more like an academic abstract than our ideal: a well-told story from somebody you know. Sector advice on how to fix this feels reductive:

- Use more "you" language.
- Keep the reading level low.
- Tell a story (but break it with asks).
- Personalize the greeting.
- Make the donor the hero.

These are pithy slogans, not useful counsel. They explain nothing about why fundraising copy so often fails to feel personal or to carry a story. And while Copy Optimizer helped quantify those problems at the sentence level—the parts of speech, the verb structures, the narrative signals, the personal-letter feel—it raised a bigger question.

If the writing is weak at the micro level, is there also a deeper problem at the macro level? Is the *structure itself* broken?

Structure That Humans Are Built For

So, we at DonorVoice did the obvious next step: We diagrammed appeals, and not a handful—seventy-eight across sectors and writers.

What we found was not an outline; it was entropy.

Paragraphs jumped from story to need to solution to need again, then to an ask, then to another ask, then back to solution, then back to story. Gratitude lines appeared in random places. Urgency was dropped in like seasoning. Dollar amounts floated with no narrative context. There was no consistent pattern except inconsistency itself.

It would be difficult for anyone to defend these outlines on their merits. They exist because no one planned them. They "just happened."

Against that backdrop, the real question became obvious: What appeal structure best produces the psychological outcomes we want?

To recap, durable giving requires delivering on three internal states:

- **Relatedness**—the donor feels emotionally connected to the people or situation.
- **Competence**—the donor believes their action will work.
- **Autonomy**—the donor feels free, not pressured, in choosing to act.

So, the task wasn't to invent a clever outline; it was to find the narrative sequence that best supports those needs.

A story comes first because it's the height of relatedness. A lived moment with a protagonist, a goal, and a struggle triggers narrative transportation. It synchronizes attention and emotion. It gives the donor someone to care about and a scene worth entering. Nothing else delivers connection as reliably.

Once the donor is grounded in a human moment, the lens can widen. The **need** section shows the broader truth behind that moment, not abstract data but the context that sets up the solution. This matters for competence; the donor must understand the problem clearly before they can believe in any proposed path forward.

The **solution** then completes the competence bridge, showing how the organization creates change and, more importantly, how the donor can extend that change. This is where the donor begins to see their action as effective, not symbolic.

Finally, the **ask** gives the donor a clear, low-friction way to act. The ask exists to maintain autonomy. It names the opportunity, not the obligation. It avoids pressure, guilt, faux urgency, and mechanical clutter. A clean, autonomy-supportive ask is the moment the donor sees themselves completing the arc that began in the story.

We call this the *Meaning Path* (Figure 6.1), and it wasn't imposed on the psychology; psychology dictated the path.

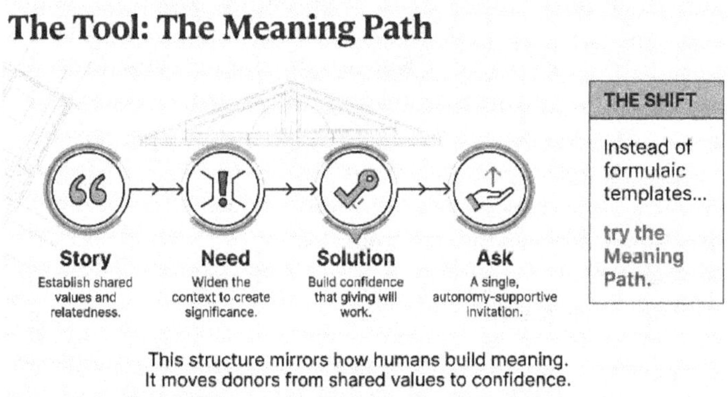

The Tool: The Meaning Path

Figure 6.1. The best sequence for writing appeals to foster reader connection.

1. **Story**—the empathy-fueled, mirroring event to create sense of connection
2. **Need**—the wider truth that makes the story's stakes meaningful
3. **Solution**—the path that makes donor action feel competent and effective
4. **Ask**—the autonomy-supportive invitation that completes the arc

This is the structure the brain uses, and it solves the chaos we saw in our diagramming.

But we needed to test it.

Experiment 1: The Survey—Why Structure Works

We pitted the Meaning Path structure against the prototypical structure we found in our sector review. Specifically, we built two versions of the same appeal (Figure 6.2):

Version A: "Frankenstein" structure (left side of image) This was assembled to mirror the most common architecture we found in the review of seventy-eight appeals: repeated switching between need, solution, and ask, with story elements fragmented or interrupted.

Version B: The Meaning Path structure (right side of image) This featured a full, uninterrupted narrative arc: character → conflict → intervention → resolution, followed by a clean transition into need, solution, and ask.

Note: The image shows the two appeals with the diagramming as an overlay for the benefit of the reader. The experiment only showed appeals, not the diagnostic overlay.

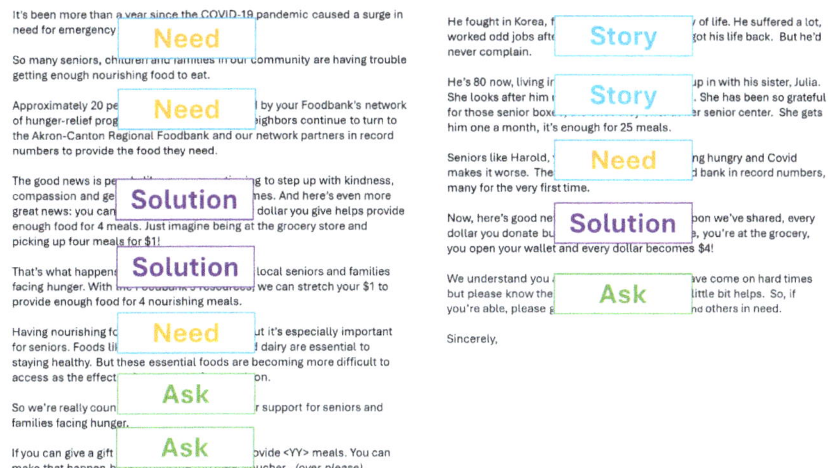

Figure 6.2. Standard control copy outline vs. Meaning Path.

We recruited donors to a hosted survey and randomly assigned them to read one version only, and immediately after reading, they answered questions about their psychological state and reaction.

What Donors Reported

Metric	Frankenstein	Meaning Path
Felt deeply or emotionally moved	54%	76%
Felt empathy	45%	55%
Felt confident their gift would help	54%	66%

Interpreting the Results: What Structure Is Doing

The story-first structure produced a sense of relatedness, competence and autonomy, the three psychological prerequisites for durable giving. The Frankenstein outline depressed all three.

But the headline is not that story makes people feel more. The headline is that structure determines whether feeling, meaning, and agency can form at all.

Experiment 2: The Marketplace

When Structure Changes, Behavior Follows

Survey data tell you whether people feel what you intend, and market tests tell you whether behavior follows. So, the next step was straightforward: Take the same two structures and let the market decide.

We ran a head-to-head in-market test using the exact same appeals we used in the survey. They were identical in purpose, audience, and channel. The difference was not the cause, not the tone, not the offer. The only meaningful variable was structure.

To recap:

Test Version—the Meaning Path Structure:

Story → Need → Solution → Ask

Control Version—Frankenstein:

Need → Need → Solution → Solution → Need → Ask → Ask

What the Market Showed

The Meaning Path structure test version produced the following:

- 15 percent higher response rate
- 34 percent higher ROI

These were gains driven by nothing more exotic than respecting how people process information and emotion.

When you follow how the mind works, donors act. Now that you know why the outline exists and what it solves, we can break down each part. We'll start where every good appeal must start: **the story**.

Story

Why Story Comes First, and Why the Appeal Collapses Without It

Writing well has always required deliberate craft. Hunter S. Thompson reportedly retyped *The Great Gatsby* just to know what writing fiction feels like. Ernest Hemingway says he rewrote the first part of *"A Farewell to Arms* at least fifty times. He also advised, "Don't get discouraged, there's a lot of mechanical work to writing."

Fundraising is no different. A good appeal is not an accident; it's an assembly of choices that create the conditions for connection and action.

Story is the first and most important of those choices, not because donors "like" stories or because it's fashionable advice but because humans processed the world through narrative long before they process it through abstraction.

Anthropologists have documented this across societies. In hunter-gatherer groups, storytelling coordinated cooperation, taught norms, and shaped group identity. Camps with better storytellers were more cohesive and more successful; people preferred to live with them, and storytellers often held elevated status. Story was not decoration; it was infrastructure.

Modern neuroscience reveals why this evolutionary pattern persists. When we encounter a story, the brain does not treat it as information; it treats it as experience. Systems for sight, movement, touch, and spatial mapping activate as if the reader were inside the scene. Motor regions fire when the protagonist acts; social-cognition networks light up when a character faces a choice. And as the story unfolds, the listener's neural patterns begin to align with the storyteller's, creating a "neural coupling" that supports comprehension, trust, and memory.

A well-told story also generates emotional chemistry associated with empathy, urgency, and prosocial motivation. Narrative transportation pulls the reader into a world where the stakes feel real and their attention is anchored. It is the most reliable way to create relatedness, the first of the three psychological needs underlying intrinsic motivation.

If the donor does not feel connected to the person in your appeal, nothing that follows—not the need, not the solution, not the ask—will matter. Story is the moment that makes the rest possible.

The Redemptive Arc That Lights Up Our Brains

Because story is experienced rather than observed, it must follow a sequence the brain recognizes. A story capable of opening a fundraising appeal always contains five elements:

- **Protagonist** (a person, place, organization, or community)
- **Hardship/crisis** (what went wrong)
- **Obstacle/ongoing struggle** (why they can't resolve it alone)
- **Turning point/hope** (what's changing or becoming possible)
- **Resolution/agency** (the positive change underway; protagonist taking action toward recovery/restoration)

This story structure, often referred to as a *redemptive arc*, matters because it models agency. Donors trust stories where change is earned, where the protagonist acts, adapts, and moves forward through a visible chain of events. But the resolution also creates space for the donor's potential impact; it shows what *could* be possible with their help.

The story doesn't directly invoke the donor; instead, it telegraphs what their contribution could achieve by showing the trajectory already in motion. When donors see a protagonist actively moving toward positive change, they can envision themselves as the force that completes that journey. The story doesn't only help the donor understand their role; it helps them feel it.

The Rules of Effective Story Craft

Start inside a moment. Skip the throat clearing, the unnecessary introduction line. Nothing kills narrative momentum faster than prefatory commentary about "challenging times" or organizational pride. Begin where something is happening; begin with the story.

Use concrete, sensory detail. Simulation depends on specificity. Replace abstract emotion ("she felt overwhelmed") with details the brain can model ("she steadied herself against the counter before speaking"). Emotion lives in action, not labels.

Keep the story in the past. The story is about what happened. The need is what is happening. The solution is what could happen. Mixing these tenses dissolves orientation.

Use dialogue sparingly and honestly. Invented conversation breaks authenticity. Real quotes can strengthen a moment, but one or two per appeal is the limit; otherwise, the narrative flow is interrupted, making the copy harder to read.

Let the resolution be earned. The protagonist should not be rescued by a miracle or by the organization emerging like a superhero. Show a chain of causes, not a leap. This prepares the donor to see themselves as part of the ongoing arc and the solution.

End with the protagonist changed. The protagonist should emerge with clarity, strength, dignity, or the ability to help someone else.

Tailor invisibly. The identity and trait insights from the previous chapter should shape tone and emphasis: steadiness for conscientious donors, warmth for agreeable donors, values and perspective for open donors, collective energy for extraverted donors, competence and calm for emotionally stable donors. Tailoring is never announced. It is felt.

These rules exist because they let the brain do what it is built to do: Enter a moment, simulate it, and care.

A Strategic Brief

This is how to bring all the elements together into one comprehensive brief that offers guidance from story to ask. This brief is invisible to the donor but essential to the writer to make the content resonate with the reader.

The Story

Charity context: Health/human services

Identity: Working parent
Rationale: Organizes values around responsibility, follow-through, protecting one's children, self-reliance, and pragmatism.

Trait: Conscientiousness (dominant)
Rationale: This audience resonates with order, diligence, preparation, and responsibility. They dislike chaos and appreciate steady, reliable support.

Moral Frame: Loyalty
Rationale: Conscientious individuals lean toward duty, obligation, standing by others, and reciprocity. "We don't walk away from people we're responsible for."

Emotion Goal: Resolve (not pity, not despair)
Rationale: Conscientious donors respond to calm, grounded determination. We want them to feel steady commitment arising in themselves—not sadness as an end point.

Story Draft:

When the clinic doors unlocked, Sara was already standing inside the entryway with her two kids. Her daughter's inhaler prescription was folded so many times it looked like a thick paper square in her hand. She kept it pressed against her palm while she counted the two backpacks at her feet—one zipped, one partly open, where a math worksheet stuck out.

She guided the children toward the check-in desk and paused. She had missed her last appointment when the late bus left them stranded two stops away, and she wasn't sure the clinic would keep her file active after a second no-show. She adjusted the strap of her bag, scanning the room for an open seat before deciding to approach the counter.

A staff member glanced up, recognized her uncertainty, and gestured her forward. "You're right on time," he said, sliding a clipboard across the desk. Sara nodded and settled the children beside her while she filled out the form, stopping twice to steady her daughter's coughing fits.

In the exam room, the physician reviewed the chart and explained that the cough was tied to unmanaged asthma—treatable, but only with routine visits. As he outlined the plan, Sara listened without interrupting, her hand resting on her daughter's back to track each breath. When he finished, she asked what the schedule would look like and whether the medication needed to be refrigerated. Practical questions, one after another.

The nurse stepped in to map out a calendar. "We can work around your shifts," she said, pointing to the openings that matched the bus routes Sara typically used. They reviewed it twice. By the end, Sara had circled three dates and slipped the paper into the front pocket of her daughter's backpack, where she knew it wouldn't get lost.

Outside, the children tugged her toward the bus stop. Sara checked the folded prescription again, now paired with a clear plan she believed she could keep. She exhaled in relief; her eyes brightened with determination. She confidently tightened the straps on both backpacks and told the children they'd return next week. Her voice was filled with certainty and gratitude.

The Story Deconstructed:

Protagonist

Sara, a working parent managing two children and real-world constraints
Why this works: Concrete person without stereotype. A reader can recognize themselves or someone they know.

Goal

Get her daughter seen, keep her file active, and secure treatment she can follow.
Goal is pragmatic—matches conscientious identity and duty-driven frame.

Obstacle

- Missed appointment history
- Risk that her file is inactive

- Bus dependency
- Children in tow
- Unpredictable shifts
- Uncertainty about medication logistics

These are steady, grounded obstacles, not melodrama, not catastrophe. *This matches the conscientious tone: real problems, solvable with diligence and structure.*

Turning Point

This was achieved by active choices:

1. **Sara's choice:** She walks to the counter despite hesitation.
2. **Clinic staff's choice:** They meet her effort with steady, structured support.
3. **Donor's hinted choice:** Their support makes the clinic welcoming and accessible.

All choices reinforce the loyalty frame. Someone showed up. Someone else stood by them. Duty → reciprocity → action.

Resolution

The change is earned:

- A clearer care plan
- A schedule aligned to her reality
- A sense of competence returning
- The confidence that routine is possible

This is an ordered path forward, exactly the emotional stance that resonates for conscientious donors.

Annotation Showing How the Story Invisibly Tailors to the Brief

Identity: Working Parent

- Tightening backpacks
- Counting belongings
- Tracking breaths

- Planning schedules
- Thinking about refrigeration

Identity appears through *behavior*, not labels.

Trait: Conscientiousness

Tone is structured, calm, methodical:

- Checking backpacks
- Filling out forms carefully
- Asking practical questions
- Reviewing the calendar twice
- Putting the paper where it won't be lost

These cues prime the donor's own conscientious worldview without naming it.

Moral Frame: Loyalty

- Staff noticing her pause and gesturing her forward
- Keeping commitments ("right on time")
- Laying out a plan that respects her effort
- Returning next week

The story shows a social contract—not a sermon about one.

Emotion: Resolve

The emotional turn is not pity.

It's steadiness—the sense that a manageable path exists.

Story Mechanics

- **Start inside a moment:** first sentence opening *at the moment of arrival*
- **Concrete details:** folded prescription, backpacks, worksheet
- **Past tense:** consistent
- **Dialogue minimal and real:** only two brief lines
- **Change earned:** logistical support + internal shift

- **End with positive change in the protagonist:** walking toward the bus stop with a plan, heading into next week
- **No boasting about organization:** competence shown through action
- **No melodrama:** grounded realism throughout
- This story works because it's crafted to respect how cognition and emotion unfold.

Need Section

Some may think *Need* in this context means "describe the problem." That mistake leads to two failure modes:

1. Data dumps—overwhelming the reader with scale
2. Despair narratives—dragging the reader into emotional quicksand

Neither delivers what the need section is supposed to create: significance, not overwhelm; moral meaning, not pity; clarity, not guilt.

A need section succeeds when it widens the lens while avoiding abrupt tonal shifts, high-level abstractions, or "organization voice." The donor should still feel they are inside the world of the story.

The problem should be framed with the desired moral frame, answering "What principle is being threatened or upheld?"

The need section also prepares the donor for the solution by showing the pattern, making the stakes clear, and establishing why structured help matters. But do not resolve anything here or imply the donor alone fixes it.

This is also where the signer "enters the frame," creating immediacy and the feeling of a human being talking directly to the donor. The shift goes from past tense (story) to present and invokes first- and second-person pronouns to sync up the writer and reader.

Lastly, the need section should not trap the reader in negative emotion; it should lead them toward the moment where they want to hear how the problem can be solved.

Here is the expanded strategic brief, including the summary from our prior story section and the need section added to the working draft.

Expanded Strategic Brief

Identity: Working parent
Trait: Conscientiousness
Moral Frame: Loyalty
Emotion Goal: Resolve
Story: Calm, grounded, steady progression

Need Summary (for writer only): Families that work hard to meet their obligations often fall out of care not because of apathy but because the system leaves them no margin for error. They need structures that adapt to their reality so that they can stay on track.

Signer: Clinic Operations Director (or program director)

Signer Rationale: A conscientious, loyalty-oriented donor responds to someone with the following characteristics:

- Understands systems
- Values reliability
- Is responsible for outcomes
- Speaks plainly
- Takes ownership

This signer can credibly say "here's what we see each day," "here's what we're solving," and "here's how you help us stay steady for families."

Voice-Transition Rule

- **Story:** Third person, past tense
- **Need, Solution, Ask:** First person ("I," "we") speaking to "you"

This mirrors a real letter, creates intimacy, and activates autonomy-supportive engagement.

Need Section of Sample Appeal

Families like Sara's come to us after doing almost everything right. They leave early, plan bus routes, juggle shifting work hours, and try to keep every appointment that keeps their children healthy. Even then, a single missed connection or an unexpected shift change can undo weeks of effort. We see this far more often than most people realize.

When a child has asthma or another chronic condition, these setbacks build on each other. Missed visits turn into unmanaged symptoms. Symptoms turn into school absences or emergency room trips. Parents who are working hard to stay on top of it find themselves starting over because the system gives them almost no room for a misstep.

As the person responsible for clinic operations, I see the same pattern week after week. It isn't neglect or indifference. It's the sheer difficulty of keeping a steady routine when the margins in a family's day are already thin. Many of the parents who come through our doors are doing all the right things, yet the path is still narrow enough that one disruption pushes them off it.

This is the need we face every day: Families who are committed, organized, and determined still struggle to stay connected to care. Not because they lack discipline, but because the structure around them doesn't flex when life does.

And unless that structure changes, families like Sara's will keep returning to square one.

Annotation of Need Section and How It Matches Brief

Shift to First Person

The signer enters seamlessly, not as an organizational figurehead, but as a responsible actor who sees the pattern firsthand. This reinforces authority + loyalty without sounding institutional.

Identity: Working Parent

Continues focusing on routines, planning, schedules, obligations—the donor "knows these people."

Trait: Conscientiousness

Steady tone, logical sequencing, structured sentences, order, and cause–effect relationships are emphasized.

Moral Frame: Loyalty

The lens is not justice or harm; it is that people who are doing their part shouldn't have to do it alone.

Emotion Goal: Resolve

The section leads the donor toward determination, not pity.

Solution

By the time the reader reaches the solution section, they understand the story at a human level and see the broader pattern that makes it significant—not in abstract terms, but in a way that makes them understand how the need shows up in everyday life. What they need next is not a tour of programs or service lines. They need a clear sense of how progress happens and how their involvement contributes to it.

The solution section exists for a single purpose: **to help the donor feel that giving is a smart, effective, choiceful action that aligns with their values and goals.**

This is the competence requirement of self-determination theory (SDT). Competence in SDT is not the organization proving it is competent. It is the *donor* feeling capable and confident that their action will produce meaningful good. They must leave this section thinking, "If I help, it will matter—I understand how my support makes a tangible difference."

That is why the solution section must not do the following:

- Shift into institutional voice
- List programs or services

- Trumpet scale, efficiency, or operational capacity
- Claim impact in the abstract
- Overload with detail or jargon

Those habits disrupt narrative transportation and push the donor into evaluation mode rather than participation mode. A strong solution section accomplishes four things.

1. It explains the mechanism, not the menu.

Donors do not need a list of everything the organization does. They need to understand the *one or two mechanisms* that turn commitment into progress. These mechanisms should connect directly to the story they just read so that the donor can picture how their support extends the arc.

Concrete, tangible examples—not program names—create competence because they feel real, actionable, and believable.

2. It translates the need into a solvable problem.

The solution should not restate the issue. It should demonstrate why success is possible and how the organization reliably achieves it. The donor needs to see the gap between what families are trying to do and what makes it possible for them to succeed. This gap should be narrow enough to feel fixable, not overwhelming.

A solvable problem increases confidence, and confidence increases giving.

3. It sticks to the first-person voice to establish trust and shared responsibility.

The donor now hears from someone accountable for the work, not a narrator. This first-person voice creates intimacy and mirrors the one-on-one nature of a real letter. It shifts the relationship from observer to participant.

The tone should remain grounded and human; the donor should feel spoken to, not spoken at.

4. It prepares the donor for the ask without preempting it.

The solution leaves the donor in a state of quiet resolve and clear understanding of how they can play a role. What you are building here is *momentum*, not closure.

- If you overclaim ("this solves everything"), the donor sees no room for themselves.
- If you underclaim ("nothing works unless you give"), you trigger guilt and pressure.
- The middle path is competence: The donor must think "I understand how this works" and "I can picture where my help fits."

The section should leave the donor feeling grounded, not exhilarated; motivated, not pushed; ready, not rushed.

Expanded Brief Including Solution Requirements

Here is the expanded strategic brief, including the summary from our prior brief and the solution section added to the working draft.

Identity: Working parent
Trait: Conscientiousness
Moral Frame: Loyalty
Emotion Goal: Resolve

Signer: Clinic operations director

Need Summary: Families that work hard to stay on top of chronic health needs often fall out of care because the structure around them is fragile. They need systems flexible enough to match the realities of their day-to-day routines.

Solution Brief (for the writer): Explain how the organization creates reliable, repeatable stability for families that are already doing their part. The solution should do the following:

- Show the mechanisms that prevent setbacks from becoming crises.
- Focus on steadiness and reciprocity, not spectacle.
- Reinforce the loyalty frame by demonstrating partnership rather than rescue.

- Show how the donors help ensure this steady work.
- Maintain the emotional stance of resolve.

The tone should be orderly, calm, pragmatic, and anchored in specifics rather than abstractions.

Solution Section of Sample Appeal

At the clinic, we have learned that families like Sara's make progress when the support around them is predictable and matched to the way their days actually work. Medical treatment is essential, of course, but the structure surrounding that treatment determines whether improvement lasts.

Our team focuses on building that structure with care. We map appointment windows to the bus routes parents rely on. For families with shifting work hours, we keep flexible blocks available so that they don't lose their place in care when a supervisor changes a shift. When someone misses a visit, we reach out to understand what happened and help them find a time that fits rather than assuming the worst.

For children managing chronic conditions, the details matter. We walk parents through medication routines until they feel confident handling them at home. When follow-up requires more coordination, we plan those steps together so that a family isn't left guessing about what comes next.

Most of this work happens quietly. It shows up in calendars, conversations, and steady routines built over time. But it is this kind of reliability that keeps families connected to care instead of slipping back into emergency visits and uncertainty. I've seen how quickly confidence returns when parents know what to expect and feel supported in keeping a routine that works for them.

That steadiness is the difference between progress that lasts and progress that fades, and it's made possible because donors help support the unglamorous parts of care, the buffer space that keeps families from falling through the cracks.

Annotation of Solution Section

How the Solution Delivers Competence

The section explains the *mechanisms* that create stability:

- Schedule alignment with bus routes
- Flexible appointment blocks
- Supportive follow-up
- Structured medication guidance

These are concrete enough for the donor to imagine the system functioning.

How the Tailoring Applies (Invisibly)

Identity: Working Parent
Every detail reflects the logic of managing routines, obligations, and real-world constraints.

Trait: Conscientiousness
The tone is measured and orderly. The focus is on structure, follow-through, predictability, and careful planning.

Moral Frame: Loyalty
The organization is steady, dependable, and reciprocal. Families show up; the clinic stands with them. Nothing in the text implies blame, pity, or rescue.

Emotion Goal: Resolve
The emotional stance is calm determination. No melodrama or despair. The reader should feel ready to continue the arc, not overwhelmed by it.

How It Sets Up the Ask

The solution shows that progress is real and made possible with support from donors.

The Ask

The ask is where everything converges. By the time the reader reaches it, they are primed for action, even before the ask is made. They already know the stakes, understand the broader pattern, and have seen how the organization responds. They also understand their role in driving change and impact. What they need now is not another explanation of the problem or a command to solve it. They need a clear, respectful invitation that allows them to complete the narrative you've built.

How to Make the Ask

When donors feel free to choose, when they don't sense pressure or manipulation, when they have been given a clear rationale for action, and when their own circumstances have been acknowledged, they are more likely to say yes and more likely to keep giving over time. High-quality motivation translates into sustained support.

But how, exactly, is this done? At DonorVoice, we compared two very different approaches to the ask. The first mirrored the prevailing sector model:

Control Ask

- Insert the ask early.
- Repeat it two or three more times.
- Layer in urgency.
- Reinforce each ask with dollar handles.

The test ask is likely what the sector calls a "soft ask," as if the choice were between weakness and firmness, with a built-in assumption that "firmness" is more effective than respectful agency.

That framing misses the point. An autonomy-supportive ask is not timid; it's psychologically intelligent. It matches how giving decisions form: through identification with a cause and the belief that one's involvement will be meaningful, not extracted.

Test Ask

- It held the ask until the end of the letter, after the full story, need, and solution arc was complete.
- It made the invitation once, clearly and without pressure, and it avoided dollar amounts entirely.

The difference in performance was decisive: The autonomy-supportive test generated 28 percent more revenue.

Why Did the Test Ask Win?

People gave more when they felt free to decide, not when they were nudged and renudged toward a preset script. The donors had room to think and feel without interruption, to follow the psychological arc to its natural end, and then decide for themselves. That freedom and respect produced more and larger gifts.

Why Not Include Dollar Amounts in the Letter?

Giving decisions unfold in two steps:

1. Will I give?
2. If yes, how much?

The letter earns step one, the reply device handles step two, and mixing them introduces cognitive friction.

There is also a deeper neurological reason. Research in behavioral economics and consumer psychology shows that currency symbols (e.g., the dollar sign) trigger activity in the insular cortex, a region activated in experiences of physical pain, disgust, and loss aversion. Studies in restaurant pricing show that removing the dollar sign increases spending because it reduces this subconscious resistance.

The same effect appears in charitable contexts: The more salient the monetary cue, the more the donor shifts into cost calculation rather than meaning making. You can feel this shift in real copy. The moment the narrative introduces amounts, the emotional frame collapses, and the reader's attention contracts.

Dollar amounts belong on the reply form, not the letter.

Why Not Repeat the Ask?

"Best-practice" copy counsel sometimes behaves as though donors are wandering through the experience, confused about what's happening, waiting for the writer to underline the word *"ask"* several times before they understand the purpose of the letter. The reality is almost the opposite.

When readers encounter repeated asks, especially ones that escalate or become more insistent, they experience it as a loss of freedom. Their instinctive response is to pull back, not lean in. Reactance isn't anger; it's the subtle cognitive move to reclaim autonomy by resisting what feels like pressure. In the "ask early and often" version, that pressure built with each repetition.

In separate research, we showed donors a range of standard nonprofit outer envelopes, and based only on seeing these envelopes, a full 84 percent said the sender was asking for money. No prompts, no hints, no exposure to the letter inside. They recognized the genre instantly because the sector has conditioned that pattern over years of repetition.

To the donor, the envelope is already the first ask.

Doubling down inside the letter doesn't create clarity but, instead, unnecessary redundancy. It tells the reader you don't think they understood, and that misunderstanding on the organization's part erodes the connection built in the story.

This envelope research included a second part, evaluating the full letter. Half the panel read a typical "best-practice" letter: multiple asks, dollar handles, urgency language. The other half read a DonorVoice version built around narrative transportation, tailored framing, a coherent psychological sequence, and a single ask at the end.

After reading, we measured three constructs tied to high-quality motivation:

- **Competence:** understanding what is being asked and feeling capable of doing it
  DonorVoice version: +2.25 compared with control
- **Relatedness:** feeling understood by the sender and connected to the people in the story
  DonorVoice version: +1.49

- **Autonomy:** feeling free to choose without pressure or manipulation
  DonorVoice version: +1.39

Readers of the multiple-ask version recognized the format, felt the demand, and responded accordingly with caution, guardedness, and for some, disengagement. Readers of the single-ask version experienced the letter as a conversation, not a transaction. They felt seen, respected, and capable—the psychological conditions that motivate durable giving rather than one-off compliance.

The conclusion is straightforward: Donors do not need repeated asks to understand what a fundraising letter is. They need an experience that makes the yes feel like their choice.

Strategic Brief for the Ask

Identity: Working parent
Trait: Conscientiousness
Moral Frame: Loyalty
Emotion Goal: Resolve

Signer: Clinic operations director

Need Summary: Families that work hard to stay on top of chronic health needs often fall out of care because the structure around them is fragile. They need systems flexible enough to match the realities of their day-to-day routines.

Solution Summary: Explain how the organization creates reliable, repeatable stability for families that arc already doing their part.

Ask Brief: Offer the donor a straightforward, respectful invitation to strengthen the reliable system that keeps families from falling out of care. Show how their involvement continues a pattern of loyalty and steadiness. The ask should feel like a practical extension of the values the reader already recognizes in themselves.

Tone: measured, responsible, grounded. Not theatrical. Not pleading. The invitation appears **once**, with no dollar amounts and no urgency cues.

Letter Copy—the Ask

I see every day how much steadiness matters for families like Sara's. When the support around them is predictable and flexible enough to match their routines, they stay on track. When it isn't, even small disruptions can undo weeks of effort.

If you are in a position to help, your support would strengthen the part of our work that keeps families connected to care: the follow-up calls, the flexible scheduling, the coaching that makes new routines possible. These are quiet pieces of the work, but they are often the difference between progress that lasts and progress that slips away.

If this approach aligns with what you value, I hope you'll consider being part of it. Your involvement would help us stay steady for the next family that walks through our doors, trying to hold their own routine together.

Thank you for considering it.

Annotation: How the Ask Delivers the Brief

Identity + Trait (Working Parent + Conscientiousness)

The ask reinforces reliability, routine, and shared effort. This tone mirrors how conscientious working parents make decisions: thoughtfully, with attention to process and practicality.

Moral Frame (Loyalty)

The ask signals reciprocity. Families are doing their part; the organization stands with them; the donor is invited to extend that steadiness. No one is shamed. No one is rescued. The relationship is mutual.

Emotion (Resolve)

The tone holds firmness without force. It encourages commitment, not sentimentality.

Autonomy

"If you're in a position to help . . ."
"If this approach aligns with what you value . . ."
These phrases give control back to the reader, which increases willingness to act. The donor is not cornered; they are invited.

Competence

The ask names the mechanisms—follow-up, scheduling, coaching—that the donor sustains. These are believable levers, not vague abstractions.

Absence of Pressure

One ask, no amounts, no fake urgency or repetition. This respects what the donor already knows and focuses on what they need: a meaningful choice.

Closing

Chapter 6 brought the two halves of effective communication together: the *raw ingredients* that make a message personally resonant and the *structure* that allows that message to land.

On the ingredient side, we introduced the resonance stack:

- **Identity** as the first constraint that explains why a donor might support a mission at all
- **Trait** as the lens that shapes tone, pacing, and the kind of language that feels natural to the reader
- **Moral frame** as the underlying logic the reader uses to judge what is right and worth supporting
- **Emotion** as the targeted feeling state that sustains motivation rather than merely provoking it

These elements work as a chain, not a menu. When these pieces align, the donor experiences the message as if it were written for them—because it was.

But ingredients alone don't produce results. They need form.

We showed how the **Story → Need → Solution → Ask** structure creates the Meaning Path, mirroring the way the human mind builds meaning. This isn't stylistic preference; it follows the psychological path required for high-quality motivation.

When you combine the stack with the structure, you move from generic messaging to precise communication. You stop writing *at* donors and begin writing *to* them.

Getting the message right is only half the equation. The other half is timing. Even the most resonant appeal fails if it arrives when the donor is exhausted, irritated, or simply not ready. Chapter 7 tackles the cadence problem—not how to send more, but how to know who is ready and when.

Chapter 7 The Cadence Problem: How Often, Not Just What

Even the most finely tuned message fails if it arrives at the wrong moment.

But most organizations ignore this and treat cadence as static: Everyone gets the same rhythm, forever. But frequency isn't neutral; it carries meaning, telling donors whether they're valued or exploited, invited or pestered. And when you get it wrong, the cost isn't just irritation; it's attrition.

The volume-machine system default is "always on." Every donor gets every campaign, all year. The assumption is simple: More exposure means more revenue.

But more often means fatigue, irritation, and shrinking loyalty. The analysis in Figure 7.1 shows the pattern in living color. The dotted blue line represents always-on fundraising, a constant. The curved red line is modeling response—it shows a natural, unmistakable human pattern of attention and inattention, on and off.

- At first, more exposure builds familiarity and response—the upslope.
- Then the effect plateaus.
- Push past it, and irritation outweighs benefit—the downslope.

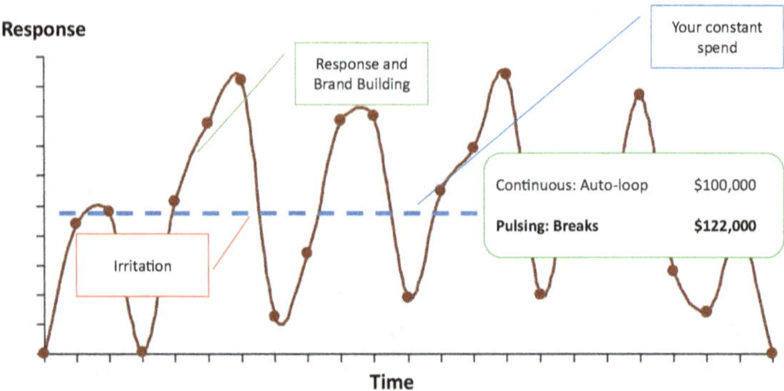

Figure 7.1. Human behavior in red against always on communication in blue

Cadence isn't a calendar problem; it's a human design problem.

The job is to decide, for each person, whether *now* is a good time to ask or whether waiting will produce more lifetime value.

There are three progressions for smarter cadence design:

1. **Pulsing:** Rotate everyone on/off using blanket scheduling (e.g., 1 month on, 1 off). It's better than the always-on approach, but it's impersonal. Still, it is much better than the always-on, ever-asking current world.
2. **Segment-Level Cadence:** Pull out donors who consistently make one gift a year (we call them *mMode-of-1 donors*) and new donors. Adjust solicitation timing based on their natural cycle and build the relationship with stewardship communications the rest of the time.
3. **Individual-Level Modeling:** Use promotion and transaction history to create a personalized, forward-looking ask plan for each donor. Factor in positive memory effects and irritation. Answer: "Should I ask this person next month or wait?"

Pulsing: Harvest Smarter, Not Harder

Pulsing is the first step away from this treadmill. Instead of swimming upstream, follow the natural human current with rotating on/off periods of activity/rest.

Off Period

A common concern is that reducing solicitation, much less going "dark," simply hands money to competitors. If you go quiet while others keep asking, donors will redirect their giving, and your organization will lose ground.

Researchers tested this directly with five large Dutch charities by varying how often each organization solicited and tracking what happened across all five brands (Van Diepen et al. 2016).

The result was nuanced but decisive. When one charity did not solicit while others did, it did lose a small amount of giving in the short term. That effect was real but brief.

What lasted was something very different. Increasing solicitation frequency did not meaningfully protect an organization from competition. Instead, it consistently reduced that organization's own future revenue. The extra gifts generated by asking more often were largely pulled forward from later appeals, leaving less to give in the months that followed.

In other words, the primary cost of over-soliciting is not that it shields donors from competitors. It is that it cannibalizes your own relationship with them. Irritation, fatigue, and disengagement are directed at the organization doing the asking, not the sector.

The evidence shows mailing less may cost you a little in the short run but mailing more *costs you much more* in the long run.

The off period isn't wasted; it's essential.

- Memory persists. Brand salience stays high even in silence.
- Irritation fades. Annoyance decays faster than memory, making the next ask feel fresher.

This is why pulsing preserves gains rather than erasing them. It's like letting a field rest so that it can produce another crop.

The On Period

When you pulse back on, the job isn't to blast a single channel harder. The job is to increase reach through variety.

People experience the same message differently if it's in different forms—short versus long, static versus video, text versus image. What feels repetitive in one mode feels reinforcing in another.

That's why the sweet spot for each pulse in the on period is four or five distinct modes. For example:

- A direct mail letter
- A follow-up email
- A short messaging service (SMS) reminder
- A digital ad to the same audience
- A phone call or short video

Each touch is another bite at the apple, but each feels different. Together, they saturate awareness without feeling like nagging.

Finding the Rhythm

In practice, this means six to eight pulses per year:

- Six if you run a month-on/month-off rhythm
- Seven or eight if you add year-end

One charity cut its mail volume from fifteen drops a year to six—a 60 percent reduction—and raised nearly the same gross revenue while growing net, thanks to lower costs and less attrition. Another cut mail volume by 50 percent; measured over two years, gross was up slightly, and net was up 23 percent. In head-to-head testing of an always-on approach versus pulsing over the course of a year, the latter was found to create 12 percent lift, on average.

Pulsing proves the point: Asking less can raise more. But it's still the same cadence for everyone. The next step is different and better.

Segment-Level Cadence: Different and Better

Brute-force pulsing is progress, but it still treats everyone the same.

Segment-level cadence starts to design around the natural rhythms of different groups. It's the walk stage, more strategic than pulsing, but still simple enough to execute broadly.

There are two behavioral cohorts worth extracting to treat differently:

1. **New Donors**—the name says it all.
2. **Mode- of- 1 Donors**—these donors only ever give once per year.

New Donors: The Mirage of "Time to Second Gift"

This is every charity's biggest pain point: 60 percent of new donors never give again.

And the sector's response? Canonizing *time to second gift* as a key performance indicator (KPI). The shorter, the better—ideally, in the first ninety days. Whole onboarding programs are designed to hammer new donors quickly until they give again.

Here's a sobering stat across more than twenty different charities with monthly solicitations:

- *Of the donors who made a second gift*, 66 percent of them stopped giving entirely after gift three, four, or five.

The "nincty-day rule" is a myth; very few donors do it, and there's no guarantee those who do are the most valuable.

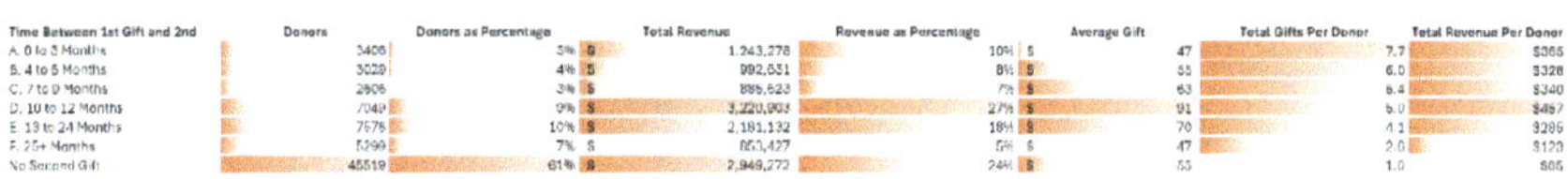

Time Between 1st Gift and 2nd	Donors	Donors as Percentage	Total Revenue	Revenue as Percentage	Average Gift	Total Gifts Per Donor	Total Revenue Per Donor
A. 0 to 3 Months	3406	5%	$ 1,243,278	10%	$ 47	7.7	$365
B. 4 to 6 Months	3029	4%	$ 992,651	8%	$ 55	6.0	$328
C. 7 to 9 Months	2606	3%	$ 886,623	7%	$ 63	6.4	$340
D. 10 to 12 Months	7049	9%	$ 3,220,903	27%	$ 91	5.0	$457
E. 13 to 24 Months	7678	10%	$ 2,181,132	18%	$ 70	4.1	$285
F. 25+ Months	5299	7%	$ 653,427	5%	$ 47	2.0	$120
No Second Gift	45519	61%	$ 2,949,272	24%	$ 53	1.0	$65

Figure 7.2. Financial results broken out by time to 2nd gift

Figure 7.2 shows a seven-year (2016–2022) snapshot of 45,519 donors and when they gave their second gift.

This organization ascribed to the early-and-often philosophy and the ninety-day edict.

- Only 12 percent of those who gave again (and only 5 percent of all first-time donors) did so in the first three months. That means 88 percent of second-gift givers didn't do it in the first ninety days, despite the aggressive effort to make it so.
- The biggest single spike in the second gift is after many charities have already declared them at risk or "lapsed": thirteen to twenty-four months.
- The best revenue per donor was the annual/anniversary giver, giving ten to twelve months after the first gift.

The takeaway: Early giving behavior is not destiny. And chasing it often does more harm than good.

A smarter new donor journey starts with a behavioral design principle: **Do less harm.**

The New Donor Journey: Designing the First Year for Motivation, Not Extraction

Most organizations treat the new donor journey as a logistical problem: how quickly to ask again, which channels to use, how to shorten time to the second gift, and so forth. That framing misses the point. The first year is not about accelerating transactions; it's about shaping motivation and increasing loyalty to the brand.

A donor's early experiences determine whether giving becomes a self-driven commitment or a short-lived compliance response. That distinction matters because only one of those sustains behavior over time.

The Jobs of the First Year

The new donor journey has two jobs, not ten: not a dashboard's worth, just two.

Job 1: Every interaction across the first year must consistently satisfy the three psychological needs introduced in chapter 6:

- **Autonomy:** Giving must feel like a meaningful, self-chosen expression of who the donor is, not a response extracted through pressure or cleverness.
- **Competence:** The donor must see clear evidence that their action worked in a way they can understand.
- **Relatedness:** The donor must feel recognized as a person with values and intentions, not a record processed in a system.

Job 2: Avoid tactics that degrade meaning.

Guilt, pressure, over-solicitation, faux urgency, premiums, and manufactured incentives all undermine the very motivation you are trying to build. They may produce a gift, but they also reliably damage the relationship.

Day 0—the Donation Moment

Day 0 is not simply the moment after someone gives. It is the first moment to anchor the gift to identity, reinforce autonomy, and establish the first evidence of competence.

Key actions:

- An acquisition message rooted in mission and identity, not pressure
- A visible but noncoercive annual recurring giving option
- Zero-party data capture embedded in the flow:
    - Your magic questions for identity
- An immediate, tailored thank-you that reflects the donor's stated motivation
- Structured CRM storage so that the data drive future behavior

Get this right, and you establish the baseline for self-driven motivation.

Phase 1—Welcome (Days 1–7)

The welcome phase is not housekeeping. It is meaning reinforcement.

The goal is to deepen belonging, reduce uncertainty, and make control visible.

- Welcome the donor into a community defined by shared values (relatedness reinforcement).
- Signal collective impact without over-claiming (competence reinforcement).
- Show them how to reach a real person, manage preferences, and explore involvement on their terms (autonomy reinforcement).
- Gently capture any missing identity or preference data.
- No ask. You are not advancing a funnel. You are stabilizing motivation.

Phase 2—Affirmation (Days 10–30)

Now the donor is asking a quiet question: Did this do anything?

This phase exists to manufacture justified satisfaction.

- Send an impact story directly linked to the kind of work their gift supported.
- Explicitly frame the gift as a wise, values-aligned decision.
- Close any remaining data gaps framed as "help us make this fit you."

Competence is reinforced when donors can see how their action mattered.

Phase 3—Community Belonging (Months 2–3)

Most organizations escalate asking here. That is a mistake.

This phase widens the relationship beyond transaction.

- Share a peer story that mirrors the donor's identity.
- Highlight collective progress.
- Offer low-effort, non-monetary participation.
- State clearly that there is no ask.
- Make opting out easy and judgment-free.

Belonging that is not contingent on giving sustains motivation.

Phase 4—Path Forward (Months 5–6)

Now the question becomes whether this fits naturally into the donor's life.

- Light brand and identity priming
- A simple, comprehensible impact report
- A sustainer or annual option framed as a natural expression of values
- Feedback on how the experience felt

You are offering paths, not prescribing behavior.

Phase 5—Anniversary Halo (Months 9–13)

Data consistently show that the strongest second-gift spike occurs around the one-year mark.

The goal here is tradition, not urgency.

- Continued identity priming
- A "Your Year of Impact" recap
- An anniversary ask framed as "make this your tradition"
- A feedback pulse that asks whether the rhythm feels right

Exit Phase—Behavioral Sorting (Month 13+)

After a year, behavior replaces assumption.

- Sort donors based on what they have done.
- Adjust cadence and content accordingly.
- Respect the rhythm they have revealed.

A new donor journey designed this way replaces early-and-often extraction with fewer, smarter, psychologically coherent experiences. It does not optimize for speed. It optimizes for durability.

Mode-of-1 Donors: Respect the Rhythm

Meet Jane. She just made her first gift to your organization. If you had to bet, what would you say happens next?

1. Odds are, Jane will never give again—that's true for 60 percent of new donors.

2. The next most likely outcome is that she gives once per year, in the same month or season as before.

This isn't a theory. It's a behavioral fact *we discovered* at DonorVoice by analyzing real donor files. We didn't set out to prove that people who give once a year give once a year—we *found* it.

We call donors who only give once a year *Mode- of- 1 donors* because they don't respond to traditional fundraising pressure. And here's the kicker:

- This segment exists in large numbers.
- It follows a dominant behavioral path.
- And it does so despite the ask-early, ask-often fundraising model.

These donors stick to their annual rhythm, even when you ask them eight, ten, twenty, or more times throughout the year. Despite repeated reminders, campaigns, and industry advice to "strike while the iron is hot," they don't budge. They give annually on their own terms. These donors don't want a second ask next week. They want to give once, with intention—and then be unsolicited until next year.

This pattern challenges the sector's golden metric: recency. We're told that the best time to ask is soon after someone has made a gift. But consider the accompanying chart (Figure 7.3) for mode-of-1 donors, which shows their recency on the horizontal x-axis and their probability of giving on the vertical y-axis.

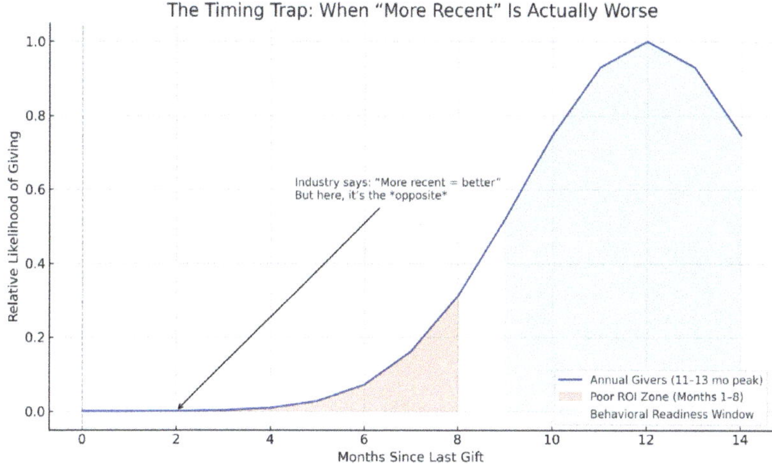

Figure 7.3. Mode of 1 donor's likelihood to give increases as get further from last gift date

Mode-of-1 donors are *more likely* to give again as their last gift becomes *less recent.*

That likelihood is maximized as they get closer to the anniversary of their previous gift, between nine and fourteen months later. That's what we dub the *Behavioral Readiness window* (shaded in blue in the graph), and it's where all solicitation should take place.

Fighting their rhythm doesn't work. These donors are intentional, reliable, and consistent in their giving—even when the organization isn't consistent in outreach efforts. What they require is a journey strategy that matches their response cycle.

But first, you need to identify them (Figure 7.4 has examples). Here's how:

- Retrieve all historical gifts.
- Group gifts by calendar year.
- If a donor has fewer than two lifetime gifts → exclude.
- If any year has more than one gift → exclude.
- If the latest gift is older than twenty-four months → exclude.

- They may have skipped a year or two, that's fine; they should be included.

Donor	*Year: Gift Count*	*Include?*	*Why*
A	2019:1, 2021:1	✅	2+ years, 1×/year when gave
B	2019:1, 2020:2	❌	One year had 2 gifts
C	2018:1	❌	Only gave once ever
D	2016:1, 2018:1, 2020:1	✅	3 years, always 1 gift/year
E	2017:1, 2018:1, 2019:0, 2020:1	✅	Nongiving year ignored

Figure 7.4. Examples of (non) qualifying behavior for Mode of 1

Once a donor is identified as mode of 1, you should go one step further: Identify their most common giving month, or as we call it, their *anniversary month*. The latter will determine their mail schedule. Without this information, you'll know you should make an ask, but you won't know *when* you should make it.

This segment isn't static. To stay accurate, you need to recalculate the counts and the anniversary months at the end of each calendar year. Regardless of your fiscal year, January is the natural reset point. Donors don't think in fiscal years. They give once a year, every *calendar* year.

Once calculated each January, this audience should be locked in for the full calendar year. The counts are expected to change over the year, but that's a known and accepted trade-off to efficiently operationalize this strategy.

Do not adjust or recalculate the counts until next January.

If your fiscal year doesn't align with the calendar, you can deal with the expected shift in counts by adding a buffer to your budgets to account for it. Then, every January, you adjust budget forecasts based on the updated counts. But know that small shifts, for example, someone gave in November instead of December—won't affect the counts. Larger shifts—such as someone giving unexpectedly in a completely different season—will be picked up the following year.

Mode-of-1 Donor Journey

It all starts with their most likely giving month. This is used to determine their ideal solicitation window. Rather than asking these donors randomly throughout the year, we concentrate our outreach when they're naturally most receptive: during their anniversary halo.

The Anniversary Halo

The anniversary halo is the three-month window surrounding and including their anniversary month: the month before (–1), the anniversary month (0), and the month after (+1).

Once you know their halo, you can plan a three-part ask: one before, one on their anniversary month, and one after.

Immediately after a donor makes a gift, they should be pulled from any future solicitations. The best time to ask them again is—you guessed it—in about a year. If suppression can't happen in time, the next message must include a mail-crossing disclaimer. If they don't give during their anniversary halo, then you can keep soliciting them.

All halo communications should do the same job: Reinforce the donor's existing pattern and gently affirm their annual rhythm—salient enough to feel personal, but never so "on the nose" that it feels gimmicky.

In direct mail, we do that with light "nods" to their annual habit in a few predictable places: the outer envelope, the footer, and the reply form headline. In an email, the same idea shows up in slightly different spots. We reference their annual pattern in the subject line and preview text. The header graphic emphasizes their impact and reinforces autonomy ("Your choice. Your rhythm").

Here are a few examples using different themes:

- **Gratitude:** Thank you for your annual commitment.
- **Competence:** Your annual gift helped achieve [example].
- **Autonomy:** You choose to give once a year—and that choice matters.
- **Respect:** We see and want to honor your rhythm.
- **Reduce Hassle:** Simplify your giving with one-click auto-renewal.
- **Experience and Outcome:** No more asks—same powerful impact on mission.

The copy still follows our Meaning Path structure like any other appeal. But the ask connects the dots and introduces annual auto-renewal as the easiest way to keep the rhythm going.

The quick response (QR) code in the direct mail and the call-to-action (CTA) button in the email do double duty: They include a simple auto-renewal prompt and take donors straight to the annual tab of the donation page.

This approach respects their rhythm while increasing relevance and response.

The Stewardship Period

We intentionally ease off outside of the anniversary halo. The goal isn't to "keep asking" just because we can; it's to reduce pressure and respect the donor's natural rhythm.

So instead of receiving regular fundraising appeals throughout the year, this group gets a lighter, more thoughtful cadence (Figure 7.5):

- **Quarterly touchpoints** that help them feel confident in the difference they make (competence) and connected to the mission and community (belonging).

Figure 7.5. Mode of 1 journey outside of halo solicitation period

- **Emergency appeals**, when needed—because responding to a true moment of urgency is a different kind of decision. And importantly, those gifts don't "count" toward their annual giving pattern.

This approach keeps the relationship warm and meaningful, without turning it into constant solicitation.

Multichannel Strategy

We take a multichannel approach—not to add noise, but to increase reach, strengthen salience, and build momentum (Figure 7.6).

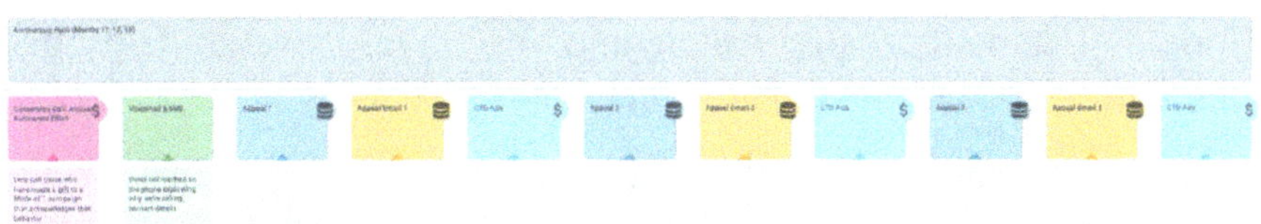

Figure 7.6. Mode of 1Journey during halo solicitation period

We kick off the anniversary halo with a phone call in the month before (–1). For records we can't reach live, we back it up with a voicemail or a brief SMS so that the touch still lands. If you want to experiment here, you could test replacing live outreach with a celebrity voice broadcast—a lower-lift way to create warmth and attention at scale.

The plan (Figure 7.7) stays consistent across the three halo months. Each month includes a combination of direct mail, email, and digital ads—different channels working together to keep the message present without feeling repetitive, as shown in Figure 7.6.

You can use reusable templates for months –1 and +1 and make small adjustments to match the month's message focus. Month 0—the anniversary month—lines up with the closest active donor mailing whenever possible, which keeps production efficient without sacrificing personalization.

Month Before (-1)	Gentle reminder	Annual gift framing and annual auto-renew option	Phone + email + digital + direct mail template
Anniversary Month (0)	Primary ask	Annual gift framing and annual auto-renew option	Email + digital + active donor direct mail
Month After (+1)	Final ask in halo	Annual gift framing and annual auto-renew option	Email + digital + DM template

Figure 7.7. Cheat sheet for Mode of 1 journey during halo window

Mode-of-1 donors are predictable and very loyal if we abide by their preferences and respect the way they want to give.

It's a mistake to think we can "fix" or "upgrade" their behavior. Our job is simpler than that: Make it easier for them to keep doing what they already do—give once a year, in a way that feels personal, intentional, and meaningful.

Individual-Level Modeling: Cadence by Donor, Not by Calendar

This is the point where we stop asking, "How often should we mail?" and start asking a more refined question: "Should we ask this person right now, or would waiting create more value?"

Traditional cadence ranks donors; personalized cadence reads them.

That shift matters because most cadence systems are still built on comparison between donors rather than understanding the individual donor. They don't ask, "What does this donor do?" They ask, "How does this donor stack up against everyone else?"

So, donors are scored, ranked, and selected accordingly. The logic is simple: The higher the value, the more contact.

The outcome is both predictable and a little perverse: Your best donors end up receiving the most pressure. It's efficient on paper—but it's not personal, and it's often not optimal. Over time, that pressure can quietly undermine the very loyalty you're trying to protect.

The Jack and Jill Problem

Meet Jack and Jill. Jack gave $50 six months ago. Jill gave $100 last week.

Jill is a better donor by every conventional measure. She gives more frequently, gave more recently, and gives at higher amounts. If you're deciding who should receive tomorrow's appeal using traditional modeling or recency, frequency, monetary amount (RFM) logic, Jill wins every time.

And that's exactly the problem.

Jill is a terrible candidate for another ask right now. Her recent gift signals connection, not readiness. Asking her again immediately doesn't increase value; it increases irritation. Jack, six months removed, is the better candidate.

Yet most systems keep mailing Jill because they compare her to Jack.

The fix is conceptually simple, even if operationally demanding: Stop comparing donors to each other. Model each donor against themselves.

What Individual-Level Modeling Actually Does

Instead of ranking donors, individual-level modeling conditions on a single person's history.

For each donor, you ask the following questions:

- When have they been solicited?
- How frequently?
- How did they behave under different solicitation rhythms?

- This requires two inputs that most organizations already have but rarely connect:
- **Transaction history**
- **Promotion history**

Together, these let you model not just *whether* someone gives but also *how asking affects them over time.* Because solicitations don't just produce a yes or no on a spreadsheet; they change Jill's behavior.

Each touch can do one of the following:

1. **Build goodwill** in the form of brand memory and readiness to act OR
2. **Create irritation and tune-out**

Both effects are real, cumulative, and measurable, and yet traditional modeling ignores both, modeling only for response, which is—always and forever—the minority outcome.

Figure 7.8 shows the math, but the governing rule is simple:

Solicit when the predicted goodwill > predicted irritation. Otherwise, hold.

$$G_{it} = \phi\, G_{i,t-1} + \gamma\, u_{it} - \kappa\, v_{it}$$

Should we mail or not? = Carryover goodwill + Mail adds to goodwill when timed to her signals − Too much mail builds irritation & inattention

Figure 7.8. Formula for deciding whether mail person or not

Why Holding Is Not Lost Revenue

One of the hardest shifts for organizations is accepting that *not mailing can be the highest-value decision.*

Irritation accumulates over time, and while each additional ask may feel tolerable on its own, together, they compound into tune-out. Messages are skimmed, then ignored, then filtered mentally before they are ever opened. Importantly, tune-out is quiet; donors rarely complain or unsubscribe in protest. They simply disappear from active participation while remaining technically on the file.

The good news is that annoyance wears off quickly once you stop applying pressure, and the better news is that the goodwill fostered from a sense of familiarity and connection lasts longer.

That means asking again too soon often does more harm than good, whereas waiting gives people space to reset without wiping out the relationship you already built.

This is where calendar-based cadence quietly fails.

Calendars assume readiness is stable. If a donor was worth asking last month, they must still be worth asking this month, right?

If an appeal cleared a profitability threshold once, repeating it feels safe. What the calendar cannot see is where a donor sits on the goodwill–irritation continuum, or whether the next ask will convert readiness or push them closer to tune-out.

Consider, though, that when Jill donates, this is her signal spiking to its highest point. Asking again immediately after that spike reliably underperforms, even when the appeal itself is strong. Over time, allowing space lets irritation decay faster than memory, creating moments where a later ask produces a higher response and larger gifts than continuous pressure ever did.

Waiting, in this context, is not inactivity; it's donor preservation.

Figure 7.9 shows the model output, letting you see whether the model understands behavior, not just averages.

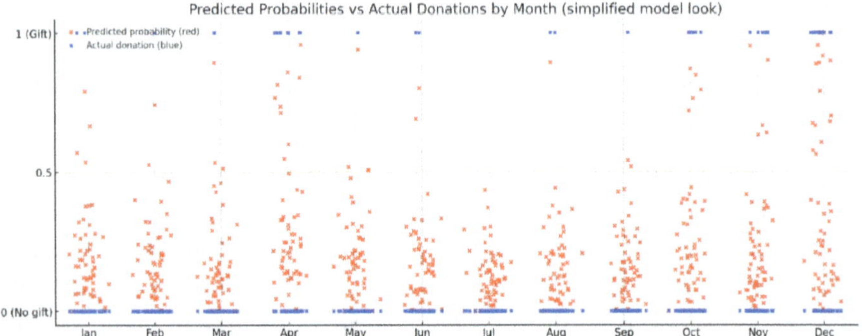

Figure 7.9. Prediction for which month to mail for each person

Each red dot is a model prediction for a specific donor in a specific month (x-axis), expressed as a probability between 0 and 1 (y-axis). For every red dot, there is a corresponding blue dot showing what happened. A blue dot at 1 means the donor gave. A blue dot at 0 means they didn't.

What immediately stands out is the structure of the blue dots. In most months, they collapse into a dense line along the zero axis. That is not a visualization artifact; it's reality—nongiving is the dominant behavior.

Now look where the red dots sit relative to that reality. Most predictions cluster well below the 0.5 (50 percent) line. That is the model correctly learning and respecting the base rate and accurately predicting "no gift" most of the time.

The more important signal is what happens higher up the axis. Red dots (donors) rise to the top as the potential for goodwill exceeding irritation goes up. These are the people you solicit in that month.

This is proof that readiness is not a static trait, and it is not driven by the calendar. It fluctuates by person and by time. The model captures that fluctuation and translates it into a forward-looking signal you can act on.

What This Looks Like in Practice

When you move from a calendar-based cadence to a donor-based cadence, the output stops looking like a schedule and starts looking like a decision system.

This all comes together in what we call the Solicitation Heatmap, as shown in Figure 7.10. Each column represents a month. Each row represents an individual donor. Each cell answers a single question: Should this person be solicited right now?

Green means yes. Red means a clear hold. Yellow means likely hold, where the model is signaling caution rather than urgency.

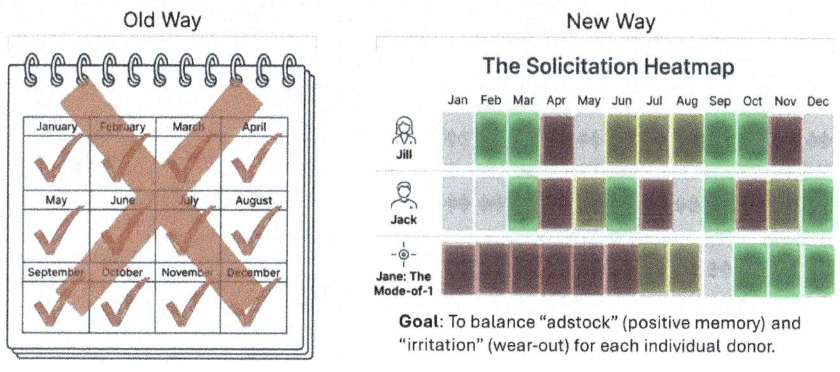

Figure 7.10. Tailoring solicitation to each person

The only objective is to maximize each donor's total giving over the next year by balancing two opposing forces: adstock, the positive memory effect of recent engagement, and irritation, the wear-out that comes from asking too often.

That goal alone forces a different kind of discipline. Some donors light up green frequently. Others rarely do. The model does not try to equalize them or smooth them into the same rhythm; it lets their behavior speak.

You Can't Make Them Up

There's a foundational error in the "ask more, make more" mindset. It assumes that giving frequency rises neatly with ask frequency, as if every additional solicitation simply adds another opportunity to say yes.

That's not how it works.

Most asks produce no gift. And the more often you ask, the more the math starts to work against you: The marginal return of each additional touch declines while irritation quietly accumulates. Eventually, you're not increasing generosity; you're increasing pressure.

Once you accept that reality, the implication is unavoidable: The problem is not persuading harder; it's deciding when *not* to ask.

Some donors are naturally responsive multiples. They will give more than once a year without friction, and additional asks don't feel intrusive—they feel relevant. Others are mode-of-1 donors. They give once, deliberately, and then they want space. Press them too often, and you don't get more gifts. You get disengagement.

These patterns are not created by strategy; they're revealed by behavior. The solicitation heatmap starts with a simple premise: Different people have different rhythms, and good fundraising respects that.

When you stop forcing everyone into the same rhythm, something counterintuitive happens. Giving becomes steadier, not scarcer. You ask less often, but at moments when a donor is receptive. Over time, revenue rises, and attrition falls—not because you worked harder but because you finally stopped fighting how people give.

Closing: Cadence Is a Signal

Cadence is not a scheduling exercise. It is a behavior signal.

Donors already have patterns. Some need bursts; some need space; some give once a year with intention. Asking more does not change those patterns.

Every time you reach out, you are teaching donors what kind of relationship you intend to have with them. Indiscriminate frequency teaches them that you either don't know them or don't respect them. Pressure-heavy cadence teaches them their value lies only in compliance.

Rhythm-aware cadence teaches them that they are seen, respected, and understood.

Pulsing works because it aligns with human attention. Segment-level cadence works because it acknowledges meaningful differences. Individual-level modeling works because it treats cadence as a decision made for a person, not a file.

The new donor journey makes this concrete. The first year is when donors decide whether giving feels chosen, effective, and personal. Cadence either reinforces that motivation or quietly erodes it. There is no neutral frequency.

Even the best cadence only works on people who are already close to giving. It can decide when to ask and when to hold. It can reduce irritation and improve timing. But it cannot create demand where none exists.

That is the limit of harvesting.

Better messaging and smarter cadence harvest today's demand more effectively. But they can only capture what's already there. Growing the pool, building the future demand that makes this compound over time, requires something the volume machine doesn't measure at all: brand. That's where Part III begins.

Part III: A Brand That Grows Demand over Time and the Metrics Required to Support It

Chapter 8
Brand: Creating Future Demand

If personalization and cadence are how you raise more from current demand, brand is how you create future demand. Brand determines who is ready to give before an appeal ever arrives. Without it, fundraising becomes a zero-sum optimization exercise, where gains come only from shifting dollars forward or extracting more from fewer people.

With it, fundraising compounds.

Brand is the half of the human operating system that is most misunderstood, not because it is unimportant but because its effects unfold slowly, indirectly, and often outside the neat time horizon of a campaign report.

Why Your Acquisition Isn't Branding

The volume-machine system assumes acquisition is brand building, and the logic is understandable. You are reaching people, and some of them are new to you. You're also introducing your name and maybe even telling a story.

In practice, two system-level barriers prevent this from being true:

1. The Selection Method
2. The Content

Selection Method

Fifteen or twenty years ago, many organizations made an immediate return on acquisition mail. Because of that cushion, data cooperatives quietly included names that didn't model well. They knew acquisition only works if the pool of prospects is continually refreshed and protected. Without new names, the ecosystem collapses.

Today, this practice doesn't exist because margins are thin, and tolerance for acquisition "loss" has collapsed. The cost to acquire is managed myopically, as if the goal were to minimize first-gift loss rather than maximize lifetime value.

Direct response is now bought to minimize cost per acquisition. Whether the channel is digital advertising, list cooperatives for direct mail, or other performance media, the system is designed to find people who are most likely to act now.

Algorithms optimize prior donors and look-alikes whose past behavior predicts near-term action. Large-scale analyses of ad delivery consistently show that most conversion-optimized impressions are served to people already familiar with the brand or predisposed to act. In one example, more than 80 percent of conversions occurred among people who were already biased toward the brand *before* the ad appeared. The ad did not create preference; it harvested it.

These acquisition engines systematically overweight those already loyal to the brand and underweight the unfamiliar, unprimed prospect audience. In short, they mostly miss the audience you need to reach with your brand spend.

Interlude: How Acquisition Mail Could Reach New People

Ironically, the brittleness of the current acquisition world exists at precisely the moment the sector is most desperate for new names.

The deeper irony is that the cooperative universe is not only a shallow pond but a shallow one with old fish. It was built for a world in which responding to mail meant writing a physical check. That world is gone. What remains is a list environment shaped by a shrinking behavioral artifact rather than the full universe of people who could plausibly care about your mission.

Those missing donors—the ones with a mission–identity fit but who will never write a check—are not bad names. They are uncultivated, unexposed, and unasked. They have never entered the system because no one ever mailed them. And the universe of new names is much larger than the current, overexposed check-writing universe.

In 2000, checks represented roughly half of all noncash payments in the United States. By 2023, they represented less than 5 percent. The decline is linear and steepest among donors under sixty. Cooperative modeling selects for a behavior that is tied to legacy payment habits.

Digital channels can and should reach these new people. Social, search, display, and behavioral targeting all matter. But this is an *and*, not an *or*. Mail can still play a role with digital-first prospects if it is designed for the way they actually behave.

Mail retains narrative weight, artifact value, and emotional presence.

What is obsolete is the assumption that the reply envelope and reply slip are the default activation path.

Commercial marketers abandoned order forms years ago because the friction is too high. Fundraising persists, forcing donors into a process that belongs to another era while ignoring the growing number of people who experience mail emotionally and convert digitally.

Matchback data already prove this. Growing numbers of mail-influenced gifts now appear online rather than in caging. Donors are doing the work for us despite the design, not because of it.

A modern acquisition package must assume behavioral diversity and provide a friction-light digital path for non–check writers influenced by mail. That means you must do the following:

- Remove the reply envelope.
- Remove the reply form.
- Include a digital activation insert designed to eliminate mental friction. Here's an illustration of one.

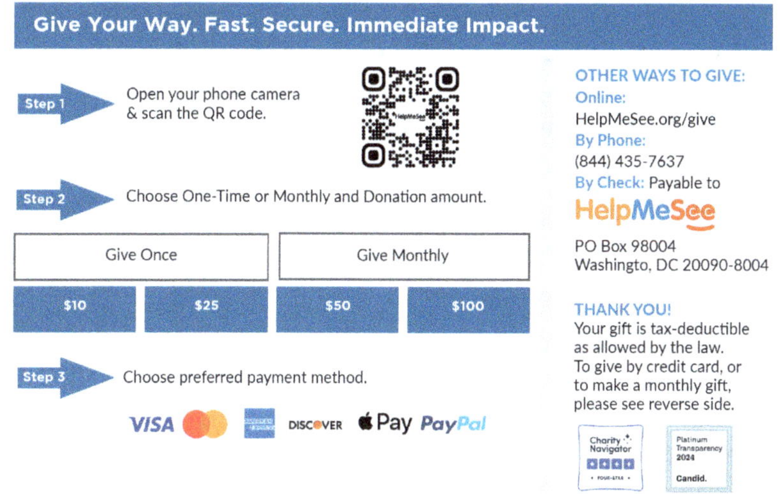

A well-designed activation card does five things:

- **It presents a single, obvious next action.** A QR code eliminates typing, remembering, and choosing among competing behaviors.
- **It removes payment hassle.** Visible card logos and digital wallets preempt "this will be annoying."
- **It signals safety.** Security language and third-party trust cues reduce perceived risk.
- **It preserves autonomy.** Multiple paths signal choice, which increases compliance.
- **It eliminates memory load.** Everything needed is on the card.

These are not cosmetic choices; they are behavioral design decisions that determine whether motivation converts into action.

Exposure, Not Extraction

New-to-file names influenced by mail but converting digitally are the names not being mailed. This means they need exposure to your brand and therefore cannot be judged on a one-drop basis. They need exposure cycles, not verdicts.

Include the same tranche for several consecutive drops, then rest those donors. Evaluate through matchback, not caging. Supplement with low-cost brand exposure ads, bought on a cost per impression versus action, to help build low-cost recognition and salience. Treat the absence of a check not as failure but as a signal that you are measuring the wrong behavior.

This is how you grow a new audience instead of endlessly recirculating an aging one.

The second system-level barrier preventing your acquisition efforts from being synonymous with branding is **the content itself.** Direct response asks for action, whereas brand asks for attention, and it's hard to have one execution do both well.

Content designed to trigger immediate behavior is often focused on urgency, need, and promotions such as premiums and matching-gift offers. Direct-response ads also tend to foreground specific programs, beneficiaries, or issues to make the case for immediate action. This concreteness narrows the decision frame and accelerates choice, which is exactly what conversion-oriented content is designed to do.

Decades of advertising effectiveness research show that this type of content produces short-lived spikes in response that decay rapidly once the campaign ends. The effect is real, but it does not accumulate. This is because collapsing attention onto the immediate problem and the immediate ask leaves little cognitive space for building broader memory associations with the organization itself. What is remembered is the issue, not who brought it to mind.

Brand has a different job, memory encoding, that operates on a different timescale. Experimental and field studies consistently show that memory formation requires attention and reinforcement over time. Content that earns only fleeting attention, just enough to prompt a click or a gift, often fails to encode into long-term memory at all. When the stimulus disappears, so does its influence.

In Figure 8.1, the gray spikes are from direct-response campaigns providing a short-term sales lift that quickly falls back to zero, with no cumulative gain. By contrast, the blue line is the result of brand-building efforts. In effect, brand advertising "feeds" the brand's long-term growth, whereas pure activation just causes temporary blips.

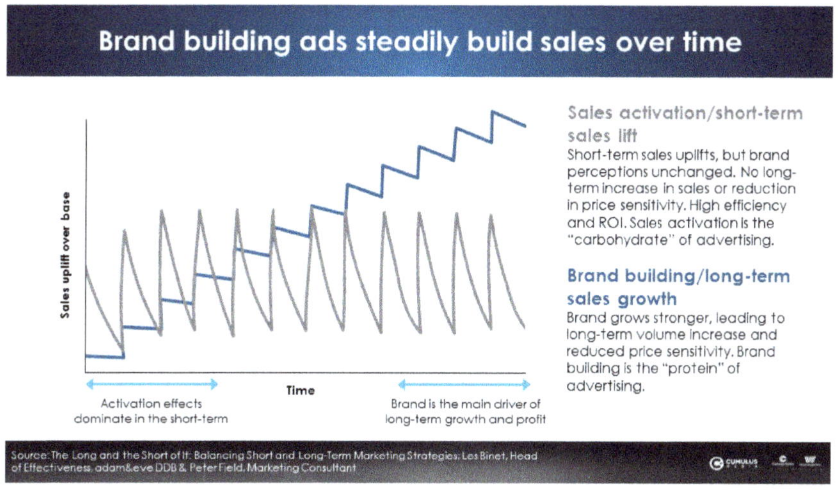

Figure 8.1. Brand spend drives sales and long-term growth

This distinction matters even more in fundraising than in consumer marketing. Giving decisions rely heavily on familiarity and trust, often more than purchase decisions do, because people are risk averse with their generosity. Brand building helps get you remembered, and people disproportionately choose what comes to mind first, particularly in low-deliberation, emotionally charged decisions like charitable giving.

Content that presses for action without building memory may raise money today, but it does little to increase the number of people who will be ready tomorrow. In some cases, it actively undermines future readiness by conditioning donors to associate the organization primarily with interruption and demand.

The Real Goal: "Know You" Versus "Heard of You"

A question: Can you name a nonprofit that protects wildlife?

Whatever came to mind first is the brand that has earned the strongest memory association for you. *Mental availability* is the technical term for this state. It does not mean admiration, loyalty, or even active interest. It means that when someone mentions the category, the organization comes to mind easily and without effort. There may be other organizations with the same mission that you'd recognize instantly if you saw their names, but they haven't made it into that first-retrieval spot.

That's the difference between people who know you and people who have merely heard of you. Those who know you can name your organization when asked, open-endedly, to list charities in your category. Those who have only heard of you cannot.

This distinction is not semantic. Across categories, longitudinal studies show that unaided recall (i.e., "know you") is strongly correlated with higher response rates, higher average gifts, and materially higher lifetime value. Donors who can recall an organization without prompting routinely outperform those who recognize it only when shown the name or logo.

Brand advertising exists to move people across that line from "heard of you" to "internalized you," and that's why it's different from direct response, which converts people who already have mental availability. Brand creates more of them.

The Three Jobs of a Brand Ad

Once the goal is clear, the mechanics follow.

A brand ad has three jobs. They are sequential, and failure at an earlier job undermines everything that follows.

Job 1: First, the ad must connect to the brand.

If people remember the story, the imagery, or the feeling but cannot name who it came from, the ad failed. Unbranded or weakly branded creative often increases category interest while benefiting the most salient competitor. Attention is earned, but ownership is lost to brands with higher mental availability. Imagine spending limited donor dollars on a campaign that people remember but attribute to a bigger, better-known organization in your sector.

Job 2: Second, the brand must connect to the category.

When someone thinks about the category, your organization should surface naturally. That is what brand strength looks like—not recall of a program name or recognition of a logo after prompting but spontaneous presence when a category becomes relevant.

The moments in life that activate concern rarely arrive as a neatly labeled "issue." They arrive as situations. For example, a conservation charity might get activated by the following scenarios:

- A wildfire dominates the news and raises questions about what is changing and what is being lost.
- A hurricane floods a coastal town and reframes abstract environmental risk as something immediate and human.
- A family plans a national park trip and encounters closures or damage that signal strain on protected places.
- A child comes home talking about endangered animals and prompts a quiet sense of responsibility.
- A drought leads to water restrictions or rising food prices.
- A photo of habitat destruction circulates without context, but not without impact.

In those moments, people are not searching their memory for a list of programs. They are orienting to a category. They are asking, often implicitly, "Who is doing something about this?" The organizations that come to mind first are the ones most likely to be supported.

This is where direct response falls short as a brand-building tool. Direct response is designed to narrow attention. It must be specific, concrete, and immediate to convert existing motivation.

Memory does not store catalogs; it stores associations. The broader and more consistent those associations, the more often a brand surfaces when the category is activated.

Strong brand advertising resists the urge to justify itself with lists and proof points. It does not try to exhaustively explain conservation. It trains memory, and over time, it ensures that when conservation enters the conversation, the organization enters with it.

Job 3: Third, the brand must develop distinctive mental associations.

These can come from positioning, but just as often, they come from visual and sensory cues that, over time, accrue as distinctive assets.

This matters because memory does not work by comparing missions. In most categories, especially in the nonprofit world, organizations sound remarkably similar when described in words. Distinctive cues solve that problem by giving the brain an easier way to recognize and retrieve an organization without effort. A symbol, color palette, visual style, or short phrase can trigger recall long before anyone consciously evaluates what makes one charity different from another.

These subtle cues matter because they operate below deliberation. People do not need to remember what you said, they only need to recognize you. When these cues are used consistently, they accumulate value over time, allowing an organization to stand apart even when its mission and programs look very similar to those of other competitors in the same category.

Two memory effects determine whether distinctive assets are doing the job: **fame** and **uniqueness**.

Fame is the extent to which people recognize the asset because they have encountered it before. It is built through repetition across time and context. Fame does not come from novelty or reinvention. It comes from showing up in a consistent way often enough for memory to form.

Uniqueness is the degree to which the asset points to one organization and no other. It reflects whether a cue is cognitively owned or shared. An asset can be famous but not unique, widely recognized but loosely associated. For brand building, recognition is not enough. The association must point back to you.

Distinctive Assets: Recognition Beats Reinvention

The World Wildlife Fund (WWF) panda is a canonical example of fame and uniqueness working together.

Figure 8.2. Evolution of panda in WWF logo

When WWF adopted the panda in the early 1960s, the choice was not the result of an elaborate branding exercise. It was pragmatic. The panda was emotionally appealing, instantly recognizable, and reproduced cleanly in black and white, which mattered in an era dominated by print. For decades, the panda often appeared on its own, not tightly paired with a logotype or explanatory language (Figure 8.2). It did not need explanation. It needed repetition.

That repetition built fame. Over time, people came to recognize the panda instantly, even without text. Mail, print, signage, advertising, and earned media all reinforced the same visual cue. The asset became familiar not because it was clever but because it was consistent.

At the same time, the WWF's commitment to the symbol created uniqueness. Because the organization adopted the panda early and used it relentlessly, the association became cognitively owned. It is difficult to think about pandas in a conservation context without the WWF surfacing alongside them. Other organizations could not easily claim the same territory without creating confusion.

What matters here is not the panda itself but the mechanism. A simple, distinctive asset, chosen for practical reasons and deployed with discipline, can generate disproportionate brand equity over time.

The Support System

Understanding the jobs is not enough. They require a support system, meaning a set of rules that make the outcome predictable even when attention is scarce and the ad is seen in passing.

How to Do Job 1: Associate the Brand with the Ad

Several execution principles follow directly from the evidence. The core idea is simple: If the viewer does not link what they saw to who it came from, you may have created interest in the cause but failed to create value for your organization.

Video

Video is powerful because it can combine sight and sound, but it has one major weakness: Most viewers do not stick around. The first seconds do most of the work, and whatever is not encoded early is often never encoded at all. So, keep the following in mind when creating video content:

- **Brand cues must appear early.** Memory encoding starts immediately. If branding is delayed until the end card, the viewer may remember the story or emotion but fail to attribute it to your organization, which means the benefit can drift to a more familiar competitor.
- **Brand cues should pulse, not hum.** A logo sitting passively in a corner for thirty seconds is easy to ignore. The goal is spaced reinforcement: brief, repeated reminders of the brand at key moments. This is how you strengthen the link between the emotional beat and the organization behind it.
- **Integrate branding into the narrative**. Branding works best when it is part of the story rather than appended to it. When the brand is treated like a separate element, it feels like an interruption. When it is embedded, it becomes part of what is remembered.
- **Use both visual and verbal naming**. Digital video allows you to show the name and say the name. That combination matters

because it gives memory two hooks, not one. Seen and heard beats seen alone.

A note of contrast: Direct mail behaves differently. Constantly repeating the organization's name in a letter can reduce response because it breaks the illusion of personal communication. In brand video content, repetition strengthens association. In direct mail, it can read as institutional and transactional.

Static Ads

Static, visual-only ads can still build brand, but they have a harder job. They cannot rely on narrative momentum or audio reinforcement, so the design must do the work quickly. The goal is immediate identification and minimal cognitive load.

To maximize brand outcomes, keep the layout simple and scannable:

- **Use a vertical, top-to-bottom structure.** This matches how people visually process content in feeds. It reduces effort and increases the chance that the brand is seen.
- **Limit the composition to three elements.** Ideally, use one image, one short line of copy, and one clear brand marker. More elements create competition for attention and reduce recall.
- **Place the logo at the top and make it meaningfully large.** If the logo is small or buried, you are relying on the viewer to hunt for it, which they will not do. The logo should be unmistakable at a glance.
- **Use distinctive, consistent colors.** The goal is not decoration; it's recognition. Color is one of the fastest cues the brain uses to identify a source.
- **Keep text extremely short.** Ten words is a good ceiling. Past that, recall drops because the viewer shifts from quick recognition to effortful reading, and most will not bother.

The test of job 1 is not whether the creative is beautiful. It is whether a distracted viewer can correctly answer a single question after minimal exposure: Who was that from? If the answer is uncertain, you did not run a brand ad; you ran a category ad that someone else can benefit from.

How to Do Job 2: Link the Brand to the Category

The goal is for your organization to surface naturally when the category becomes salient in everyday life. The key is that these moments exist outside of, and independent of, any charity. Like identity, they are already there, already meaningful, already capable of triggering attention. Your job is to attach your brand to them.

In the brand research literature, these moments are often referred to as *category entry points*, meaning the cues and situations that cause someone to start thinking about a category at all. They are the raw material of category association.

There are two ways to make the attachment, and strong brands often do both.

1) . Show the category entry point in the creative.

This is the simplest route. You repeatedly depict the real-life cue that activates the category, with clear brand ownership, so that later, the cue itself starts to bring your organization to mind. This is basic cue-based memory: Retrieval works best when the cue is present at memory encoding, not introduced later.

For nonprofits, the practical rule is to lead with the situation, then let the brand ride with it. Do not lead with a program explanation or an internal priority. Lead with the moment the donor already recognizes.

Examples of entry points across categories:

- Health: A diagnosis moment, a scan appointment, a treatment routine, a headline about a breakthrough
- Hunger: A grocery receipt shock, a pantry shelf running low, long lines in a local news segment, holiday meal planning under strain

- Children: Back-to-school season, a child struggling to read, foster care stories, a parent searching for safe after-school options
- Justice: A ruling, a policy change, a documentary night, a viral clip that reframes fairness or protection
- Animal welfare: A rescue moment, a disaster displacing animals, a family considering adoption

You are not trying to cover all these category entry points in one ad. You are trying to make the category entry point unmistakable and your brand's relevance to it memorable.

How This Looks in Static Ads

A static ad must do its work at a glance, so the entry point needs to be visually obvious. Use a single clear scene that instantly signals the category, paired with strong brand cues. If the viewer must read to understand what category the ad is even about, the ad is too slow for the job.

How This Looks in Video

Video gives you sequencing. Use that advantage: Open with the entry point immediately and then bring the brand into the first few seconds so that the viewer does not remember the moment but lose the owner. You can still be emotionally subtle, but the category cue must be fast and legible.

2.) Put the brand where the entry points occur.

The second route is environmental. Instead of only depicting the situation, you show up in the places and time windows where the situation is likely to be active.

In commercial marketing, this mechanism is familiar. Corona has intentionally maintained a long-running association with the beach, treating "the beach" as a category entry point that the company wants to own and making the brand feel like it belongs whenever you are at the beach.

The nonprofit analog is not "be everywhere." It is "be present in the situations that reliably activate the category," especially the ones you can predict, such as the following:

- Predictable seasons (hurricane season, back-to-school, winter hardship)
- Cultural calendar moments that reliably cue the category (major awareness months, legislative sessions, community events)
- Physical locations where the category is top of mind (trailheads and visitor centers for conservation, clinics for health, schools for children's causes)

You can do this lightly—the point is not domination; it's repeating the pairing between the entry point and your brand.

When job 2 works, you stop needing to reintroduce yourself every time. The category cue does the activation, and your organization shows up as a default option because you have trained memory to link you to the moments that matter.

How to Do Job 3: Build Distinctive Assets That Create Fame and Uniqueness

There is a common instinct to try to win on brand with positioning statements that suggest the brand is doing unique work or familiar work in a unique way. That is the hardest place to win because categories are crowded, and words and claims blur together.

Distinctive assets win at a different level. They give memory something simple to grab, store, and retrieve under time pressure. They also help you get noticed in cluttered environments, where even your own creative can distract from the brand.

1. Start with what counts as a distinctive asset.

Distinctive assets are the non-name elements of identity: color, font, logo, characters, celebrities, jingles, icons, and other sensory cues. When paired with the brand name, they increase the chance people notice the brand among the clutter. When they become strong enough, they can sometimes do the work even without the name.

The practical implication is not "be creative"; it's "be identifiable quickly."

2. Aim for fame and uniqueness, in that order of logic.

A distinctive asset must have both characteristics:

- **Famous:** People recognize the asset because of repeated exposure.
- **Unique:** It evokes your organization, not a cluster of similar charities.

Uniqueness is the more important of the two because fame that points to multiple organizations does not create ownership. This is where "category ownership" fantasies usually die. Categories tend to be shared, already occupied, and cognitively crowded.

3. Build a small set of cues, not one lonely logo.

It's easy to think the logo is the brand, but strong identities use multiple cues that work together: a symbol, a color system, a typographic style, a repeated phrase, sometimes an audio cue.

Using multiple identity elements together can create richer processing without demanding more effort from the viewer. In practice, that means you should design for a "bundle" of recognition: If someone misses the logo, the color and the icon still do the work.

4. Reduce internal clutter so that the asset can be seen.

Clutter is not just competitors; it is also everything you put inside the ad. Too many visual elements can distract from noticing the brand at all.

Simplicity is a requirement; if the asset is not processed, it cannot become famous. If it is not consistently processed, it cannot become unique.

5. Make repetition nonnegotiable.

Fame is built through repeated exposure across time and context, which requires discipline.

The common failure mode is "refreshing" identity elements to keep things feeling new internally. That is a donor-hostile move because it resets learning. The managerial move is to treat key assets like rules, not suggestions. If your creative system allows exceptions, you will end up with a brand that is always being reintroduced.

6. Use the grid to decide what to emphasize, what to fix, and what to drop.

The distinctive asset grid, a quadrant plot with Uniqueness on the X-axis and Fame on the Y-axis, is useful because it forces a decision.

- **Use or Lose:** High fame, high uniqueness. Use relentlessly.
- **Invest:** Unique but not yet famous. Keep it and build exposure.
- **Avoid:** Famous but not unique. It cues competitors as much as you.
- **Test or Ignore:** Low on both uniqueness and fame. Either revise the execution or move on.

This placement of distinctive assets into the grid should not be left to intuition; it should be empirically validated, as discussed next.

How to Empirically Validate Your Distinctive Assets—a Case Study

An international animal welfare organization wanted to increase its presence in the US conservation and animal protection landscape. The organization's instinct was a familiar one: To win mindshare in a crowded market, the organization believed it needed to own a category (e.g., domestic animals, animal welfare, animal rights, wild animals). The logic felt sound: If the organization could claim a clear thematic lane, donors would know what it stood for.

The problem is that categories are not owned in the donor's mind. They are shared, blurry, and already saturated with strong incumbents.

At DonorVoice, we conducted research to identify which distinctive asset candidates could realistically work and which are already cognitively crowded.

Design:

- Recruit prospective donors from the target market.
- Present a set of candidate "assets" that includes both traditional identity cues (symbols, icons, colors, taglines) and any proposed category claims.
- For each element, capture two things:
    - **Fame:** The percentage of respondents who recognize the element as something they have encountered.
    - **Uniqueness:** Among all the linkages people make, the share that points to the client rather than competitors.

When we tested these category claims, the results were predictable and instructive. Each category showed low uniqueness (left-hand quadrants in Figure 8.3); donors associated those ideas with multiple large organizations, often more established ones. Even when a category had moderate fame, meaning people could link it to several charities, almost none of that linkage pointed uniquely to this organization. The mental real estate was already taken.

We then tested something the client initially viewed as secondary—a simple, literal, distinctive asset embedded in the organization's name and identity: a paw print. Unlike the abstract category claims, the paw print had two advantages that categories never do. It was concrete, and it was repeatable; it said what it was without explanation.

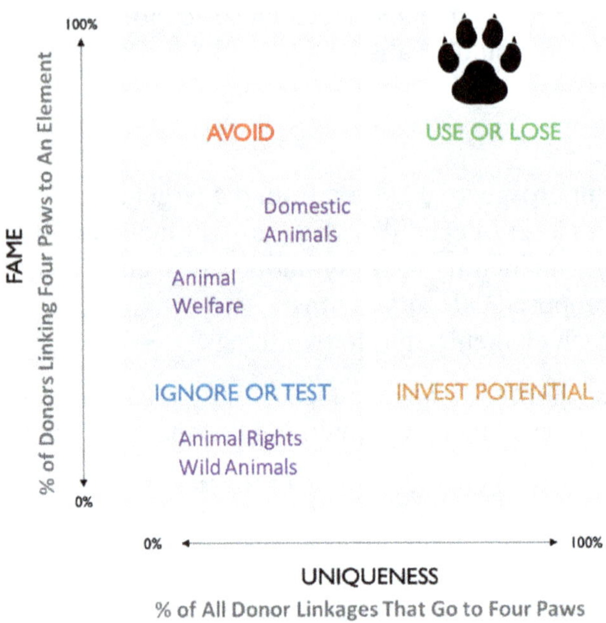

Figure 8.3. Distinctive Asset Grid for a conservation charity

The paw print performed differently. It was a highly recognizable image, and because it directly cued the organization's name, it was inherently self-referencing. That linkage advantage mattered. The asset did not need to compete at the abstract category level. Uniqueness was effectively built in—not because the symbol was clever but because it collapsed recognition and attribution into a single mental step.

In grid terms, category claims were stuck in shared territory. The paw print had a realistic path to high uniqueness, and with repetition, it had a path to high fame.

This is the quiet power of distinctive assets. When an element naturally points back to the brand, every exposure does double duty. It builds memory and ownership at the same time, something generic category claims rarely achieve, no matter how often they are repeated.

The decision that followed was straightforward: Stop trying to "own" abstract categories and commit to an asset that can accumulate fame and uniqueness over time.

Distinctiveness does not come from saying something no one else says. It comes from owning something no one else consistently uses.

Putting It All Together: An Ad-Testing Framework for Brand Ads

Putting media spend behind anything is expensive, especially if it's not doing the intended job(s). This research methodology is a cheap, quick way to evaluate whether brand advertising execution delivers the three jobs under realistic attention conditions.

Most ad testing quietly cheats by giving participants too much attention: full-screen exposure, long view times, forced reading. This design avoids that.

Design:

- Recruit prospects into a controlled study environment.
- Randomly assign participants to one of two ads:
    - **Control:** Typical nonprofit brand execution
    - **Test:** An ad built to follow the principles in this chapter
- Show the ad inside a mocked-up Facebook feed, placed in a right-side banner alongside unrelated content.
- Expose the feed briefly, for only a few seconds; then remove it and immediately field questions.

Question flow (mapped to the three jobs):

1. **Unaided brand recall:** "Which organization, if any, did you just see?"
2. **Aided brand recognition:** Confirm recognition without giving credit for guessing.

3. **Category recall and association:** Only for those who show any brand recognition, test whether they link the brand to the intended category.
4. **Distinctive asset linkage:** Test whether the key asset in the creative is attributed to the brand, not simply noticed.

What this methodology solves:

It forces the ad to earn attribution under the same conditions in which donors encounter real brand ads: low attention, competing stimuli, no intention to memorize. That makes it a better test of whether you are building memory structures, not just producing pleasing creative.

Figure 8.4 shows the results of an ad that abides by all the principles outlined (left) tested against the control ad (right). The evidence-based ad outperformed the control on all three jobs: brand recall, category recall, and linkage to distinctiveness.

Figure 8.4. Ad testing results for brand ads

This measurement methodology is portable. Any organization can use it to evaluate whether its brand advertising is building ownership, category connection, and distinctiveness.

The Memory Engine

Brand is not aesthetics or messaging polish; it's a cognitive system. We refer to this system as the **Memory Engine**.

The Memory Engine (Figure 8.5) describes how future demand is created and depleted over time. Planting builds memory structures; harvesting converts readiness.

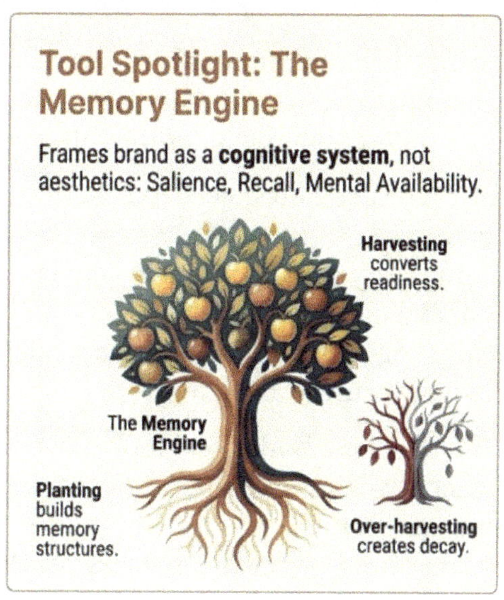

Figure 8.5. The Memory Engine

Overharvesting depletes the system by exhausting attention and increasing irritation faster than memory can replenish demand.

When brand activity is working, it strengthens salience, recall, and mental availability. More people know you and think of you unprompted, which makes them more ready when the ask eventually arrives.

When harvesting consistently runs ahead of planting, the engine degrades, and familiarity turns into fatigue.

Cadence optimization becomes an increasingly fragile attempt to extract revenue from a thinning pool.

Creating your own Memory Engine does not require massive budgets. It does require consistency, reaching beyond the familiar, and creative discipline over time.

Why Brand Takes Time, and What Is Changing Under the Hood

Brand does not change behavior immediately; it changes memory, and memory must accumulate before it alters response rates. The subtle activity taking place out of sight includes the following:

- Cognitively, repeated and spaced exposure strengthens retrieval pathways.
- Socially, familiarity spreads through conversation, recognition, and cultural presence.
- Mechanically, algorithms and response models only adjust once behavior changes.

Short-term tests often make brand spend look like a bad bet. As shown in Figure 8.6, when two similar organizations are compared, one investing in brand (purple) and one not (blue), the first few months typically show weaker direct-response metrics for the brand investor. Cost per dollar rises, and on a dashboard, it looks like a failed test (chart on the left).

But extend the time horizon, and you reach the exact opposite conclusion: Brand spend improves your direct-response metrics (chart on the right). The same direct-response tactics suddenly work better—not because they changed but because the audience did. More people recognize you, trust you, and feel ready, so the same ask converts better.

This is also why brand rarely shows up cleanly in attribution: It does its work before attribution begins. Attribution systems credit the final touch, not the accumulated memory that made that touch effective.

Short measurement windows punish brand for doing its actual job.

Brand Building Takes Time

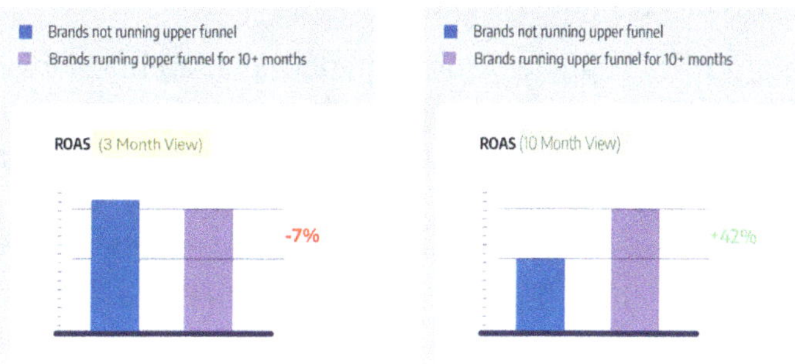

Figure 8.6. Brand spend takes time to positively impact financial metrics

The Compounding Effect

Appeals decay, lists churn, and tactics wear out. Brand accumulates.

Every effective brand exposure increases the likelihood that the next appeal feels familiar rather than interruptive or foreign. Over time, this raises responsiveness and lifetime value without increasing pressure.

Brand is not optional because it is the only lever that grows the future donor pool rather than extracting more from the one you already have.

You do not need new dollars to begin this work.

Brand investment comes from your existing direct-response budget. The only real decision is how much to reallocate. Smaller organizations will move cautiously. Larger, well-established brands can afford to move more. That imbalance is real, but it is not the core problem.

The deeper issue is double jeopardy.

Decades of marketing research show a consistent pattern: Smaller brands suffer twice. They have fewer buyers, and those buyers are less loyal. Larger brands benefit twice: more buyers and slightly higher repeat behavior. This is not because large brands are smarter, more creative, or more differentiated. It is because they are more mentally available. People are more likely to think of them, recognize them, and choose them.

Fundraising recreates this dynamic.

Smaller nonprofits begin with low mental availability. Fewer donors think of them spontaneously, recognize their signals, or remember them when giving opportunities arise. In response, they rationally lean harder into direct response because it is the only lever that reliably produces immediate revenue. But this survival strategy triggers the second penalty. By prioritizing harvesting almost exclusively, these nonprofits prevent brand growth that would reduce their disadvantage in the first place.

The brand strength of larger organizations makes every appeal more efficient, which creates surplus cash flow. That surplus allows them to invest further in brand, increasing mental availability even more. The weaker brand associations of smaller brands force short-term tactics, and short-term tactics lock in weak brand.

This is not a theory or a fairness issue. It is a structural outcome of how memory, attention, and budget constraints interact. The trap tightens when organizations confuse survival with growth and mistake short-term efficiency for long-term progress.

The Misconception That Keeps Smaller Organizations Frozen

The final misconception is the belief that brand only works once you are already big. The evidence says the opposite.

One of the most robust findings in marketing science is that growth comes primarily from increasing buyer penetration, not from increasing loyalty. Small brands do not grow by squeezing more value out of the same donors. They grow by being noticed and chosen by more people, even if those people are only lightly engaged at first. Brand investment does exactly that, increasing the probability that an organization comes to mind at all.

Why Brand Matters More When You're Small

Brand effects are not linear. A small increase in mental availability produces a disproportionately large impact for smaller organizations. When you are rarely thought of, moving from almost never to occasionally remembered changes everything. Direct response optimizes conversion among people already paying attention. Brand changes who pays attention in the first place.

This is why modest, consistent brand investment is not wasteful for smaller nonprofits. It attacks the first half of the double-jeopardy problem by expanding reach and recognition, which in turn improves the efficiency of future appeals. Even small amounts of planting make harvesting less expensive and less exhausting over time.

The mistake is waiting for surplus before investing in brand. Surplus is the outcome of brand strength, not the prerequisite. Organizations that delay brand investment until they feel safe are effectively waiting for a condition their own strategy prevents from ever arriving. Brand does not eliminate double jeopardy, but it is the only lever that weakens it.

Knowing what to invest in is only useful if you can measure whether it's working. The volume machine's reporting tools were built to evaluate harvesting—they are the wrong instruments for a system designed for growth. Chapter 9 builds the right scoreboard.

Chapter 9
Measurement That Supports Growth

Nonprofits do not drift into short-termism because fundraisers are shallow, boards are stupid, or donors are irrational. They drift because the volume system dashboard makes short-termism feel like the responsible choice. Conversion rate, cost per acquisition, ROAS, and cost to raise a dollar create a world where the only "real" outcomes are immediate and attributable, and the only "smart" decisions are those that win inside a narrow window.

That scorecard isn't neutral; it's a strategy engine.

Rewarding only what you can attribute cleanly this week, or month systematically underinvests in what creates next year's demand. And then, once next year arrives and demand is weaker, the scorecard will "prove" you were right to underinvest because the only tactics left that still show a clean return are extraction tactics.

This is the starvation loop in spreadsheet and dashboard form.

Why Efficiency Metrics Become Growth Limiters

In marketing science, there is a long-standing distinction between activity that captures existing demand and activity that creates future demand. The evidence base behind that distinction is substantial, and it repeatedly shows that an overemphasis on short-term activation reduces long-term performance because it underfunds brand building, mental availability, and the creation of future buyers. Sustained growth requires balancing short-term activation with long-term brand building, and the two play different roles.

Nonprofits have a parallel problem, but with an added handicap. We have trained donors and boards to scrutinize overhead and fundraising efficiency ratios, which makes organizations even more allergic to investments that do not produce instant, attributable revenue. The literature on overhead aversion documents that donors reduce giving when they believe overhead is higher, even when overhead funds the very capacity that makes impact possible. That pressure pushes nonprofits toward underinvestment in capability and long-horizon growth.

This is why cost-to-raise-a-dollar logic is seductive and dangerous. It encourages an organization to prefer tactics that look efficient in a short window, even if those tactics shrink the future donor pool. It also turns fundraising into a contest of superficial cleanliness, where the best-looking line items win even when the organization is slowly hollowing itself out.

The metrics designed to protect short-term cash flow often undermine long-term revenue growth. By focusing only on immediate, attributable returns, they hide compounding effects and systematically over credit harvesting from existing donors.

Organizations respond rationally to what the scorecard rewards, but the future donor pool quietly shrinks. The sector does not choose decline, but it measures in a way that makes decline the rational outcome. So, we need a scorecard that can see compounding.

The New Scorecard: BRAIN

The Tool: BRAIN Framework

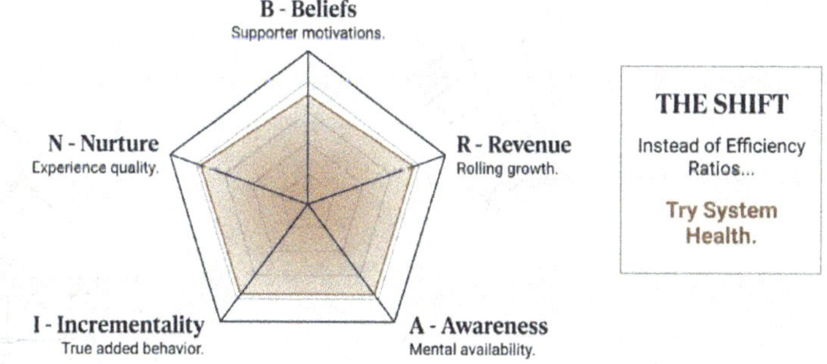

Figure 9.1. The BRAIN measurement and operating system for growth

BRAIN is a full-system measurement framework (Figure 9.1) built around what causes durable giving. It isn't a dashboard; it's an operating system for growth, designed to make long-term effects measurable, trackable, and defensible inside organizations that are otherwise pulled toward short-term proof.

BRAIN stands for the following:

- **B: Beliefs** (understanding supporter motivation)
- **R: Revenue** (growth as the North Star)
- **A: Awareness** (building mental availability and brand memory)
- **I: Incrementality** (understanding causal lift, not credit-claiming)
- **N: Nurture** (measuring and acting on supporter experience)

The key design rule is simple: Whereas the old model tries to explain growth by staring backward at the last touchpoint in the journey, BRAIN measures the upstream drivers that create that last step, then uses revenue as the ultimate arbiter of whether the system is working.

If any metric says you are "doing great" while revenue growth is shrinking, you are rearranging deck chairs.

B: Beliefs

Most fundraising measures are behavioral—opens, clicks, gifts, recency, frequency, average gift. Behavioral data are indispensable, but they are incomplete. They tell you what someone did. They do not tell you why they did it, how they see themselves, what meaning they attach to giving, or what trade-offs they are making emotionally and financially.

Behavior is an output; motivation is the system that produces it.

When an organization relies exclusively on behavioral data, it eventually does what every behavior-only system does. It optimizes what is easiest to move in the short term. That usually means urgency, pressure, and repetition. These tactics can generate revenue today while quietly degrading the psychological conditions that sustain giving tomorrow.

This is not a failure of intent; it's a failure of instrumentation, and primary research is the missing instrument.

Primary research measures the psychological ingredients that sit upstream of behavior and that never appear in a CRM: identity, motivation, perceived agency, trust, and relationship strength. Analyzing behavior without these inputs is like trying to explain flight using only wind speed.

The resistance to primary research in fundraising usually comes dressed as hard-nosed realism. You have probably heard some version of this (real) claim:

The only research you can trust is actual response to real fundraising. Surveys can reveal interesting information, but they can't uncover real motivation. Only behavior can do that.

What that argument lacks in accuracy, it makes up for in certainty.

The reality is exactly the opposite. You cannot understand the *why* of an action by relying only on behavioral data. Behavior is ambiguous without a psychological context. Lengthy time-on-page measures might indicate deep engagement, or they might indicate confusion. Nonresponse might signal disinterest, or it might reflect bad timing, channel mismatch, or a donor who would give under different conditions. A gift to "Program X" does not tell you whether the donor cared about that program, responded to a narrative, felt a moral obligation, or simply recognized the brand.

No amount of torturing of behavioral data will tell you why someone took an action. At best, it allows you to guess.

Skepticism toward surveys usually has a different origin. Many people have experienced terrible survey research, and they are right to distrust it.

A lot of surveys are not research for insights; they're questionnaires producing attractive charts and very little strategic leverage. They ask people directly what they "care about," analyze the results descriptively, and then mistake frequency counts for insight. That approach is not just weak; it's dangerous when organizations act on it.

The failure here is not surveys; it's methodology.

- There are right and wrong ways to ask questions.
- We know, empirically, how people read, process, and answer survey items.
- Question formulation is a science, not an art. It is governed by the same rigor as statistical analysis, and when that rigor is missing, the data are garbage.

You cannot measure motivation, intent, trust, or loyalty without attitudinal data. Measuring only the behavior is like measuring temperature by watching people sweat.

Many of the most important constructs in fundraising cannot be measured directly. They must be measured indirectly, using sets of statements that together capture a deeper construct. This is why single-question shortcuts like Net Promoter Score are of limited value. Complex psychological phenomena require multiple items and proper scale construction.

This is why the common myths about surveys persist. They are based on bad implementations.

Remove the False Choice

The false choice between "what donors say" and "what donors do" collapses under scrutiny. The real question is whether what donors say and what donors do align, diverge, or change over time. Often, how someone feels about an organization is a better predictor of future behavior than the fact that they did not give on the last appeal.

The right approach is not choosing between surveys and behavior; it's integrating them.

Primary research becomes powerful when it is designed with an analytical plan in mind, not as a stand-alone insight exercise. Attitudinal data should be joined with transactional and engagement data, then modeled together. This is how organizations move from description to explanation.

- When psychological measures are combined with behavioral data, organizations can answer questions that behavior alone never can:
- Which supporters are intrinsically motivated versus externally pressured?
- Which identity signals explain giving?
- Which experiences strengthen long-term commitment rather than short-term response?

A survey that lives in a slide deck is insight theater. A survey that feeds models, segmentation, cadence, and message design is a strategy.

Primary research is not optional because without it, every downstream optimization is riddled with guesswork.

R: Revenue—a Single North Star That Ends Internal Self-Deception

Revenue matters. Growth matters. What doesn't matter is isolated success divorced from system health.

The volume-machine system tracks revenue obsessively and yet still fails to track and be guided by the only question that matters: *Are we growing or shrinking over time?* The reason is not lack of data; it's the absence of a clear, nonnegotiable growth calibration at the top of the organization.

In the BRAIN framework, revenue is the North Star not because it explains performance but because it constrains interpretation. It is the metric that prevents local wins from masquerading as progress.

The Growth Score

Revenue is a simple, continuously updated growth score:

- **Revenue Growth Score** = Revenue over the last 365 days ÷ Revenue over the prior 365 days.

- **Donor Growth Score** = Unique donors over the last 365 days ÷ Unique donors over the prior 365 days.

For both, if the score is above 1, the organization is growing. If the score is below 1, the organization is shrinking.

Everything else in the measurement system lives underneath this constraint.

Why This Calibration Is Essential for Leadership and Boards

Boards and senior leaders are often presented with a steady stream of positive news. A strong campaign. A record Giving Tuesday. A channel that "beat forecast." A test that "won." Each of these stories can be true in isolation and still be irrelevant to the organization's long-term health.

It does not matter how many records you break on individual days, campaigns, or channels if the overall revenue base is contracting. In fact, those moments can distract, and this is where the growth score does its real work by removing the ability to confuse activity with progress.

Ending the Tyranny of Local Optimization

Without a growth constraint, organizations default to local optimization, celebrating improvements in conversion rate, ROAS, or cost per dollar raised, even when donor counts are eroding and long-term revenue is flat or shrinking. The volume-machine model allows this because it treats efficiency as success, regardless of trajectory.

The growth score makes that impossible.

If rolling revenue or donor growth is below 1, no efficiency metric can override that reality. A campaign did not "perform well" if it extracted efficiently from a shrinking base. A channel did not "work" if it improved ROAS while accelerating donor loss. Those are signs of controlled decline, not excellence.

This is not a judgment of staff performance; it's a diagnostic about system health.

Revenue as a Constraint, Not a Target

The most important shift here is conceptual. Revenue is not the thing to optimize directly. It is the constraint within which all other metrics must make sense.

The beliefs, awareness, incrementality, and nurture elements of BRAIN exist to explain *why* the growth score is moving. They provide the levers, and revenue provides the verdict.

That is why revenue is the North Star of the BRAIN system.

A: Awareness—Measuring Mental Availability, Not Exposure

Awareness is a familiar but imprecise proxy in the brand world for what really matters: mental availability. Mental availability is the probability that your organization comes to mind quickly and easily in a relevant giving context.

Decades of research in marketing science show that brands grow primarily by increasing mental availability, not by persuading people who already care to care more. People choose what is easiest to think of and easiest to recognize.

Why Exposure Is the Wrong Proxy

Impressions, reach, and frequency measure what you bought, not what changed. They tell you how often something was shown, not whether it was encoded into memory.

You can reach millions of people and still be mentally absent. You can also be mentally available to far more people than your paid reach would suggest if your assets are distinctive and consistently deployed.

This is why awareness measurement must focus on memory, not media.

Mental availability has two core components.

The first is **unaided recall**. Do people think of you, without prompting, when they think of the general cause category your charity occupies?

This is the strongest indicator that your organization has been internalized.

The second is **aided recall (recognition)**. When people see your name, do they know who you are? This matters because recognition reduces friction. People are more likely to engage with what feels familiar.

Both matter, but they aren't interchangeable. Unaided recall reflects ownership of mental territory; aided recall reflects accessibility once attention is directed.

Distinctive Assets and Attribution, Not Aesthetics

Earlier in the book, we discussed distinctive assets as the building blocks of brand memory. This is where they become measurable.

The question is not whether your assets look good. The question is whether they reliably point back to you and not to others. Fame without attribution is wasted exposure. Recognition without ownership is noise.

This is why awareness measurement must assess not just whether an element is recognized but also whether it is uniquely linked to your organization. If multiple charities trigger the same association, you do not own it, no matter how much you like it.

Branded Search as a Practical, Continuous Signal

One of the barriers to measuring awareness is the assumption that it requires expensive studies or frequent tracking. That belief is outdated.

One of the simplest and most underutilized indicators of mental availability is branded search.

If brand activity is working, people should search for you more often. Not because they saw an ad five minutes ago but because your organization has become more mentally accessible. When a giving opportunity arises or when curiosity is sparked, your name comes to mind.

Tracking branded search volume over time using tools like Google Trends provides a free, continuous signal of this effect. It is not a perfect measure of brand-building success, but it's directionally useful, especially when examined alongside periods of brand investment. Related, new user sessions on your website should rise—another useful, free metric.

If you invest in brand and branded search but new user sessions remain flat, you should be skeptical. If branded search rises steadily, especially relative to category trends, it is strong evidence that memory is being built.

This matters because branded search and new users often lead to other beneficial outcomes. They're early indicators that future demand is being created, even if revenue effects lag.

Awareness Is a System Input, Not a Vanity Metric

The reason awareness belongs in the BRAIN framework is not because it feels good to be known. It is because awareness changes the economics of fundraising.

Higher mental availability lowers the cost of response, increases the probability of engagement, and reduces the need for urgency and pressure. It makes direct response work better without changing the ask.

This is why awareness cannot be evaluated in isolation. It must be read alongside incrementality and revenue. A rise in awareness without any downstream effect may indicate weak execution. A rise in awareness followed by improved incrementality and efficiency is evidence of planting paying off.

The volume-machine dashboard has no place for this signal, so it dismisses it as "soft" or unprovable. The BRAIN framework treats awareness as what it is: a leading indicator of future revenue capacity.

I: Incrementality—Are We Creating New Behavior or Just Taking Credit?

Most fundraising reporting answers the wrong question with great confidence.

- Wrong question: which channel got the gift?
- Right question: did this activity create behavior that would not have happened otherwise?

A lot of fundraising activity sits on top of a base rate because some supporters were already going to give. They might give after an email, a retargeting ad, a search click, or a direct mail piece, but the intent existed before the touchpoint. If your measurement system cannot separate "would have happened anyway" from "caused by the intervention," it will systematically over credit activity and under detect noise. That is how the volume-machine model convinces itself that more fundraising equals more growth.

Why Attribution Fails as a Proxy for Incrementality

Attribution systems are built to assign credit, not to establish causality. Last-touch, first-touch, and multiple-touch models all share the same flaw: They assume that because a touchpoint happened before the gift, it caused the gift.

Often, it did not.

A donor who sees a retargeting ad and then gives may simply be giving because they were already ready. A donor who clicks a paid search ad for your brand name is rarely being persuaded into caring. They are expressing preexisting intent. A donor who responds to a mail piece may be acting on a long-standing commitment, not a specific package. Attribution models cannot distinguish activation from creation. They only tell you where behavior was observed.

This is why high-volume systems produce impressive dashboards. More touches create more opportunities to claim credit for the same underlying intent. If you add a new channel like SMS and evaluate it using the SMS platform's claimed ROAS, the volume machine will treat any observed gifts as additive. But the real question is whether those donors would have given without SMS and whether the new channel changes total behavior or just rearranges where credit gets assigned.

Incrementality exists to break that illusion.

Incrementality Is About Counterfactuals

True incrementality asks: what would have happened if we had not done this?

You cannot answer that by looking harder at the same data. You answer it by constructing a credible comparison between a world with the intervention and a world without it. That is why incrementality is experimental by nature. You need a control condition, not a smarter attribution model.

There is a second distinction that changes how organizations think.

Incrementality is usually a channel or system question, not a creative preference question. Before you debate which ad is "better," you should first ask whether the channel or category of spend is producing any incremental value at all.

Common Approaches to Incrementality Testing

1. Individual-level randomized tests

This is the cleanest method when you can do it. Randomly assign individuals to receive or not receive an intervention and then compare the outcomes.

In fundraising, it is most practical for direct-response tactics where you control exposure and can reasonably prevent contamination. It is less practical for brand and awareness efforts where spillover is the whole point and individual isolation is unrealistic.

2. Holdouts and channel suppression tests

This is the workhorse approach most nonprofits can run. The idea is straightforward: Remove a channel and see whether total outcomes change.

There are two versions.

A. Full suppression: Turn the channel off for everyone

This is the simplest test and often the most persuasive internally.

You stop spending on the channel, then observe whether total revenue, donor counts, or target behaviors decline over a meaningful window (e.g., three to six months).

This is especially useful for channels that claim very high ROAS and are therefore most likely to be taking credit rather than creating new behavior. Retargeting and paid brand search are the usual suspects. If you turn off retargeting and revenue does not move, the "ROAS" was mostly attribution theater. If you turn off paid brand search and total revenue does not move, you were paying to intercept intent that would have found you anyway.

The limitation is that this design is vulnerable to confounds. If something else changes during the same period, you cannot cleanly separate cause and effect. It is still useful as a blunt truth test, but it is not the cleanest experiment.

B. Partial suppression: Withhold the channel from a portion of the audience

This is the more controlled version.

You deliberately withhold the channel from a subset while the others continue to receive it, then compare outcomes. Because both groups live through the same period, this approach reduces the risk that seasonality, news, or a campaign change explains the difference.

It is also safer operationally. You do not have to risk a full stop across the whole program, and you can scale the test based on tolerance.

Both versions answer the same core question: Is this channel creating incremental behavior, or is it mostly capturing credit for behavior that would have happened anyway?

3. Geo-split testing for system-level questions

Geo tests exist for the things you cannot randomize at the individual level, especially brand.

The clean way to think about geo is this: You are not testing a brand ad in isolation. You are testing what happens when the overall fundraising system in a set of markets gets an added investment, typically brand or upper-funnel media, while everything else stays business as usual.

- **Control regions:** Normal direct-response activity across channels.
- **Test regions:** The same direct-response activity plus the added brand investment.

Then you compare outcomes over time. The outcome is not ad recall. It is system behavior: donor growth, revenue growth, and whether direct-response performance improves because readiness improves.

Geo tests are messy by design, but that is the point. They preserve real-world conditions. If you are trying to understand whether brand spend creates future demand that makes your other fundraising work better, geo is often the most practical experimental tool.

4. Marketing mix model (MMM)

An MMM can be useful when you have enough data and the capability to do it well. For many nonprofits, it is heavy, assumption-laden, and easy to misread. Treat it as a complement when you have maturity, not as the first tool you reach for.

A Better Decision Sequence: Prove the Lever Before Polishing It

An incrementality mindset operates with two rules:

1. First, test whether a channel or category of spend is incremental.
2. Then and only then, optimize within it.

This mindset changes behavior. It skips declaring winners and losers among creative variants before proving the channel is doing anything new.

If retargeting shows a 6:1 ROAS, that is not a victory. It is a reason to test. If paid brand search looks like the best performer in your mix, that is not a victory. It is a reason to test. High reported ROAS is often the signal of credit capture, not true creation.

Same with the volume machine's favorite move: Add a new channel like SMS, see donations attributed to it, declare it additive, and expand. Incrementality would ask the uncomfortable question: Did SMS increase total giving, or did it simply reroute gifts that would have come through email, mail, or web?

Where Things Can Go Wrong

There are three ways in which incrementality testing can be unintentionally sabotaged:

1. **Testing windows that are too short**
   Brand and experience effects rarely show up on the same timeline as direct response. If your window only captures immediate response, you are measuring activation, not creation.
2. **Treating short-term efficiency softening as failure**
   Incremental growth investments can temporarily lower channel-level efficiency metrics. That does not mean the intervention failed. It may mean the system is shifting from pure harvesting toward demand creation.
3. **Optimizing before proving incrementality**
   Teams spend months debating creative and channel mix while never answering the foundational question of whether the lever works at all. That is how organizations become busy, not effective.

Why Incrementality Matters More Than Optimization

Incrementality prevents confusing activity with impact. It exposes when "more fundraising" is simply extracting from the same pool of intent. It creates the evidence needed to defend long-term decisions to boards and executives who are otherwise trapped by short-term dashboards.

Most importantly, it shifts the organizational question from "Which version won?" to "Did anything change?"

That is the only question that matters for growth.

N: Nurture—Measuring Experience and Commitment, Not Output

Experience Measurement

Nurture is not how many non-solicitation touchpoints appear on a calendar. Nurture is the quality of the experience a supporter has when they encounter you.

Birthday cards, newsletters, and impact reports feel like nurture because they require effort, and they seem different from the appeals. But the supporter's experience is not what is sent; it's what they *feel* when interacting with you. And experience, not frequency, is what determines whether motivation strengthens or erodes over time.

That is why nurture cannot live as a soft concept or a vague best practice. It belongs inside the measurement system. If you are not directly measuring how supporters experience your communications, you will not see decay as it happens. You will only see the outcome months later, when retention drops, response rates soften, and churn quietly accelerates. By then, the damage is already done, and every intervention is reactive instead of preventative.

Why Retention Is the Wrong Starting Point

Retention is a lagging outcome. It tells you that something went wrong, not what went wrong or when it started. Optimizing nurture by watching retention metrics is like trying to improve health by monitoring mortality rates.

What matters is the psychological state that precedes retention.

Decades of motivation research point to a consistent conclusion: Sustained engagement depends on whether interactions support or frustrate basic psychological needs. SDT identifies three such needs that are especially relevant in fundraising contexts: autonomy (sense of control), competence (sense of impact), and relatedness (sense of connection).

When these needs are supported, motivation becomes more intrinsic and resilient. When they are repeatedly frustrated, motivation becomes fragile and dependent on external pressure. This is not a theory in search of application. It is one of the most replicated findings in motivational psychology.

Nurture measurement exists to detect this shift early.

Brand Commitment Measurement

A critical blind spot in measurement is the failure to distinguish between commitment to a cause and commitment to an organization.

Many supporters feel deeply connected to a mission while remaining weakly attached to any specific charity. In crowded categories, this is the norm, not the exception. People care about animals, the environment, justice, or health. That does not mean they feel a relationship with *you*.

This is why the **commitment score** matters.

Commitment measures the strength of the supporter's psychological connection to the organization itself, not just agreement with the mission. It captures whether supporters see the organization as "one of us," whether it occupies a meaningful place in their identity, and whether the relationship feels reciprocal rather than extractive.

This distinction is well supported by organizational identification research, which shows that identification with an organization predicts loyalty-like behaviors above and beyond satisfaction or agreement with goals. Translating that insight into fundraising is not optional if you want to understand resilience.

Without a commitment measure, organizations routinely overestimate their strength by confusing cause passion with brand equity.

Measuring Nurture Properly

Effective nurture measurement is not a long annual survey. It is a lightweight, continuous listening system embedded into real supporter touchpoints.

A mature nurture system measures three things together:

1. **Experience quality**, through autonomy, competence, and relatedness measures
2. **Commitment**, through identity and relationship-strength indicators tied to the organization
3. **Context**, by linking these signals to recent interactions, cadence, and channel exposure

This allows organizations to see not just *that* experience is changing but also *why*.

Just as importantly, the analysis cannot stop at reporting. A bar chart showing "average satisfaction" is operationally useless. The value comes from variance and pattern: which supporters feel pressured, which feel disconnected, which feel ineffective, and how those experiences correlate with behavior over time.

Closing the Loop: Stop Reporting; Start Improving

Supporter feedback should not sit in a report; it should route the next action.

A bar chart showing "average satisfaction" is operationally useless. The value comes from metrics that offer actionable insights and from looking at individual variance and patterns: which supporters feel pressured, which feel disconnected, which feel ineffective, and how those experiences correlate with behavior over time.

The defining feature of the nurture element in the BRAIN framework is that it closes the loop. This is where your logic matrix belongs.

- When a supporter signals low autonomy, the system should reduce pressure, slow cadence, and restore choice in the next touch.

- When a supporter signals low competence, communications should clarify impact, simplify decisions, and reinforce efficacy.
- When a supporter signals low relatedness, the next interaction should emphasize recognition, belonging, and human connection.

Crucially, these responses are not generic "stewardship." They are tailored interventions based on how the supporter experienced the relationship.

This turns nurture from a cost center into a profit center. It prevents burnout, reduces silent disengagement, and protects future revenue by maintaining the psychological conditions for giving.

If you are not measuring experience and acting on it, you are flying blind. You will eventually see the consequences in retention and revenue, but by then, the damage is already done.

How BRAIN Becomes a Cultural Operating Rule

BRAIN is not a reporting framework; it's a discipline. And like any discipline, it only works if it is shared and enforced across the organization.

This is not just a board issue. It is a senior leadership and staff issue, which makes it a culture issue. Every organization already has a measurement culture, whether it names it or not. You can see it in what gets celebrated, what gets defended, and what gets quietly ignored. If teams are rewarded for local wins, they will optimize locally. If leaders allow flattering metrics to stand in for system health, the system drifts, even when everyone is acting in good faith.

The purpose of BRAIN is to remove that drift by creating a better view of reality.

One Scoreboard, No Escape Hatches

When BRAIN is working, there is only one question that comes first: Is the system growing or shrinking?

The growth score answers that question. Everything else exists to explain it, not override it. No campaign, channel, or team gets to declare success without reconciling their results to the outcome.

This changes behavior quickly. Staff members stop optimizing in isolation because isolated optimization stops earning credibility. Senior leaders stop arbitrating between competing dashboards because the system provides a constraint. Boards stop reacting to anecdotes and start asking better questions.

BRAIN does not eliminate disagreement, but it eliminates confusion about what matters.

Shared Accountability Across Roles

Each role in the organization interacts with BRAIN differently, but no role is exempt from it.

- Boards use the growth score to anchor oversight and resist the pull of short-term stories.
- Senior leaders use BRAIN to allocate resources, protect long-term investment, and prevent efficiency theater.
- Staff teams use it to understand how their work contributes to system health, not just local performance.

This alignment matters because growth is not produced by any one function. It emerges from the interaction between understanding supporters, building memory, creating incremental behavior, and sustaining motivation over time. A culture that only sees the last step will always sabotage the steps that come before it.

The shift is complete when the organization stops asking:

- Did this work?

  and starts asking:

- Did this change anything?

When that shift takes hold, the familiar pathologies of volume-machine fundraising begin to loosen. Short-term wins stop crowding out long-term thinking. Brand stops being treated as indulgence. Research stops being treated as optional. The donor experience stops being invisible.

The organization goes from celebrating moments to managing trajectories, not because anyone was persuaded by a framework, but because the scoreboard made a different set of decisions rational.

That is the real purpose of measurement. Not to justify what you already did, but to make better choices hard to avoid. Because once you can see what is real, the old playbook becomes indefensible.

Conclusion: What Comes After the Volume Trap

The volume machine didn't happen by accident. It emerged from a reasonable assumption—if asking works, ask more—and was reinforced by an incentive system that rewards activity, a reporting system that only rewards the short-term, and a sector-wide rush for ever greater efficiency. It's a trap precisely because it looks like strategy while it's running.

But the data have been telling a different story for years: shrinking files, falling retention, donors who give once and vanish, and organizations that mail more and raise less. These aren't isolated failures—they are the predictable output of a system optimized for the wrong thing.

The alternative this book proposes isn't a new tactic. It's a different operating model; one built on a single insight that the volume machine ignores: people do not give because you ask. They give because giving means something to them. Your job is to understand what that something is and make it easy for them to act on it.

That understanding begins with identity—knowing which version of themselves a donor brings to your mission. It deepens with the resonance stack: the personality traits that shape how they process information, the moral frames that tell them what is right and worth supporting, and the emotional posture that turns recognition into action. When these four elements align in a message, giving stops feeling like a response to a request and starts feeling like an expression of who the donor is.

Cadence is the other half of the personalization equation. The question is never simply how often you ask—it is who is ready, when, and what kind of contact they need between asks to remain motivated rather than worn down. The new donor journey, the mode-of-1 framework, individual-level modeling: these aren't theoretical constructs. They are practical tools for replacing the calendar with something smarter.

Brand is what makes the whole system compound over time. Every direct-response dollar you raise is harvesting demand that already exists. Brand is how you grow the field. The three jobs of a brand ad—associating the organization with the category, linking it to giving moments, building distinctive memory assets—are not marketing abstractions. They are investments in future revenue that the volume machine's dashboards will never show you, because the volume machine doesn't look that far.

And BRAIN is how you govern all of it honestly. Beliefs, Revenue, Awareness, Incrementality, Nurture. Not as separate reports, but as a single integrated view of whether the system is growing or shrinking. When organizations adopt BRAIN as their operating standard, the familiar pathologies begin to loosen—not because anyone was persuaded by a framework, but because the scoreboard made a different set of decisions rational.

The shift this book describes is real and it is possible. It doesn't require a budget you don't have. It requires a willingness to question the model you've been handed and build something better in its place.

Ask less. Ask better. Raise more.

About the Author

Kevin Schulman is a social scientist and serial entrepreneur, the former by choice the latter by virtue of being unemployable. He ended up in fundraising by accident and stayed because too much of it didn't make sense.

Before founding DonorVoice, he spent years in the commercial sector building models that linked what people believe and feel to what they actually do. Not what they say in surveys. Not what they click once. What they consistently do over time. When he looked at nonprofit fundraising through that lens, the gap was hard to ignore.

The field had become highly optimized around activity, not understanding. It knew how to ask. It did not know why people give.

DonorVoice was built to close that gap. The name was deliberate — chosen specifically to avoid his initials (a small act of restraint he remains proud of) — and to anchor a different starting point: that giving is a human behavior shaped by identity, emotion, and context, and that ignoring those forces is the fastest way to make fundraising less effective over time.

Fourteen years later, that idea has been tested across organizations, channels, and economic cycles. Some of it worked immediately. Some of it failed first. All of it contributed to a clearer picture of what actually drives giving and what quietly erodes it.

This book is the result of that accumulation. It took six months to write and fourteen years to have something worth writing.

He is the founder of DonorVoice and DVCanvass, and serves as Managing Editor of the Agitator/DonorVoice blog, where he continues to question assumptions the sector tends to treat as settled.

www.ingramcontent.com/pod-product-compliance
Lightning Source LLC
LaVergne TN
LVHW010903110826
845149LV00005B/1456

* 9 7 9 8 9 9 5 7 6 4 3 1 1 *